MAKING DESIGNER | Mixed-M
AND Memory Jewelry

First published in the United States of America by

Quarry Books, a member of
Quayside Publishing Group
33 Commercial Street
Gloucester, Massachusetts 01930-5089
Telephone: (978) 282-9590
Fax: (978) 283-2742
www.quarrybooks.com

Library of Congress Cataloging-in-Publication Data

Powley, Tammy.
   Making designer mixed-media and memory jewelry : fun and experimental techniques and materials for the home studio / Tammy Powley.
      p.   cm.
   ISBN 1-59253-314-0 (pbk.)
   1. Jewelry making. I. Title.
TT212.P6833 2007
745.594'2—dc22   2006026689
                                  CIP

ISBN-13: 978-1-59253-314-5
ISBN-10: 1-59253-314-0

10 9 8 7 6 5 4 3 2 1

Design: Dutton and Sherman Design
Photography: Allan Penn
Illustrations: Michael Gellatly

Printed in Singapore

MAKING DESIGNER Mixed-Media AND Memory Jewelry

FUN AND EXPERIMENTAL TECHNIQUES AND MATERIALS FOR THE HOME STUDIO

TAMMY POWLEY

GLOUCESTER MASSACHUSETTS

QUARRY BOOKS

CONTENTS

CHAPTER 5
Found Objects and Natural Materials

CHAPTER 6
Mixed-Media Jewelry Gallery

SECTION II
JEWELRY PROJECTS

CHAPTER 3
Ephemera and Memory

CHAPTER 4
Collectibles and Souvenirs

INTRODUCTION

Beads and findings are usually the first materials that come to mind when making jewelry. Craft stores and online vendors offer a plethora of beads, findings, and other related components. Bead stringing, wire work, and bead weaving are some of the more popular jewelry construction techniques, and usually, this is where beginners start their jewelry crafting experience. But what if you want to create a piece of unique wearable art that truly reflects your personality?

More and more jewelry makers and fashion-conscious creative types are pushing the boundaries of traditional approaches to jewelry making. Bead stringing and wire work, long the staples of many jewelry designers, are still important elements to the mix, but a new wave of jewelry designers are beginning to explore other choices as they discover that they don't need to stick with traditional supplies and techniques to make jewelry. They are mixing, layering, and adopting a combination of techniques from other craft forms and joining them with jewelry making.

This movement into exploratory jewelry, known as *mixed-media jewelry*, is an evolving trend. The home artist has discovered methods for incorporating elements that reflect her own personal style by literally integrating and mixing media. Glass, fibers, found objects, and paper are examples of alternative media for jewelry making. A movie ticket, a glass button, a scrap of ribbon, or a bottle cap—as mementos from the everyday, these bits and pieces reflect our lives and their meaning adds another layer to a finished piece of jewelry. When combined with traditional jewelry-making techniques, the home jewelry artist is able to create unique jewelry.

For this book, a number of mixed-media artists have come together to present an exhibition of distinctive jewelry designs, and they share their clever, yet surprisingly simple, methods. Developed as a portal to the world of mixed-media jewelry, this is a guide for both beginning and more advanced artists. The Mixed-Media Techniques chapter provides step-by-step instructions along with illustrations for the mixture of methods used, including stamping, collage, fiber applications, and conventional jewelry procedures. The Projects section—organized into Ephemera and Memory; Collectibles and Souvenirs; and Found Objects and Natural Materials—shows how to take these techniques and develop beautiful and unusual jewelry designs. Throughout the pages, you will find more tips for crafting and collecting unusual elements for your jewelry.

Now it is time to flex your creative muscles. Explore unique possibilities of crafting wearable jewelry art while learning traditional jewelry-making methods. Learn to work with alternative jewelry media such as paper, fibers, and found objects, to find a balance between the conventional and the curious. When you find this balance, you will discover your own signature approach to designing reflective jewelry that mirrors your personality.

CHAPTER 1

Tools and Materials

To get started making mixed-media jewelry, you will need some essential tools and materials, as well as an understanding of some jewelry-making basics and other common crafting techniques. This section discusses some of the fundamental elements you will need such as glues, brushes, and hand tools, but this is just a guide to assist with the initial setup of your work area or to expand your current studio. Do not limit yourself to what is listed here. Almost any kind of crafting supply can be used to create jewelry. This section is merely a good place to start. When using a product for the first time, make sure you read labels and follow safety procedures prescribed by manufacturers. Many materials, such as glues and glazes, can be toxic if handled incorrectly.

Pliers

Basic jewelry-making techniques are most easily completed with a few styles of pliers:

Round-nosed pliers: These are used for making rounded loops in the wire. Since these are a specialty tool used for making jewelry, you won't find these at the hardware store. They are available at most craft stores and jewelry supply vendors.

Flat-nosed pliers: Also called chain-nosed pliers, flat-nosed pliers are useful when working with wire and connecting different jewelry components. Look for a pair that is not textured on the inside of the nose.

Nylon-nosed pliers: You can probably live without these, but they are very handy for straightening wire. If you plan to work with wire regularly, then they are worth the investment. Again, these are made especially for wire jewelry work, so look for a pair at your local bead shop, craft store, or favorite online jewelry-making supplier.

Crimping pliers: These pliers are specially designed to attach crimp beads. While you can also flatten a crimp bead with a pair of flat-nosed pliers, the crimping pliers give a more finished look to the crimp bead and rolls the crimp bead when securing, rather than flattening.

Cutting Tools

Utility knives, craft knives, paper cutters, scissors, and wire cutters are all useful for cutting paper, fibers, wire, plastic, and Fome-Cor.

Make sure you have a collection of cutting tools available and keep them in good condition. Wire cutters should be flush-cut so that you get a smooth cut to your wire work. For utility knifes, keep extra blades on hand, and replace the blades regularly. Dull blades can damage paper and other materials

Wire cutters

Wire

An extremely versatile element when designing jewelry, wire is useful for connecting pieces, making components—such as clasps—or adding a nonfunctioning decorative element.

If you plan to use wire for a function such as connecting pieces or a clasp, then precious-metal wire such as silver, gold-filled, or copper are good choices. Wire sized from 18 to 22 gauge (1 to 0.65 mm) is a good range to have available. If you plan to use wire for embellishments, consider using colored wire. For detailed information on making wire jewelry, see *Making Designer Bead and Wire Jewelry* (Quarry Books, 2005).

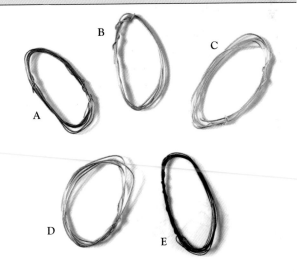

An array of wire: (A) copper (B) galvanized (C) sterling silver (D) gold-filled (E) coated colors

Adhesives

For the mixed-media jewelry maker, glues and adhesives can be some of the most helpful supplies on hand. Try out a few different types to see which brands you prefer, but try to have the following on hand:

Jeweler's cement: Many manufacturers sell glue or cement for jewelry making. (G-S Hypo Cement is shown.)

Tacky glue: Extra-thick tacky glue is good for metal, paper, wood, glass, and plastics.

E-6000: A unique adhesive formulated to meet high-performance industrial requirements, it has exceptional adhesion to wood, metal, glass, fiberglass, ceramics, masonry, and concrete; great for heavy or hard-to-glue components.

Glitter glue: Usually found in small tubes that can be used like a pen, glitter glue is useful for decorating and adhering paper-weight items.

Fibers

Ribbon, leather, yarn, hemp, and other fibers are useful for creating simple cords to hang pendants or charms. They can also make attractive embellishments.

Decorative Papers

Look for interesting papers in scrapbook and craft stores. Other decorative papers can include wrapping paper, magazine clippings, and pages from old books.

Scrapbooking Supplies

Many embellishments and tools are suitable for jewelry. Eyelets come in handy because they allow you to create holes for connecting pieces and findings such as ear hooks and clasps:

Eyelets, eyelet setter, and hammer: An eyelet is a round piece of metal (or sometimes plastic) that secures a hole, normally made in paper, but also sometimes in fabric. An eyelet setter, when tapped with a hammer, flattens and secures the eyelet to the hole punched in a piece of paper. You can often purchase eyelet kits that include a hammer as well as the setter, paper punch, and eyelets.

Eyelet pliers: These pliers offer another simple method for setting eyelets. They are simple to use—just refer to the manufacturer's instructions.

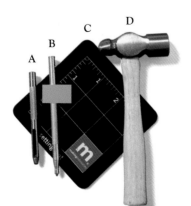

(A) Hole punch (B) Eyelet setter
(C) Setting mat (optional) (D) Hammer

Stamping Supplies

Rubber stamps can transform plain paper, wood, glass, and other materials. Along with the stamps, you may need any combination of the following related supplies:

Ink pads: At a minimum, you want a black ink pad but, of course, ink pads are available in all kinds of colors. If you plan to try any embossing, then you will want to have pigment or embossing ink on hand.

Embossing powder: Use embossing powder with pigment inks and a heat gun. Powders are available in various colors, both opaque and transparent.

Baby wipes: These are really handy for immediate cleaning of stamps.

Heat gun: Also referred to as an embossing heating tool, a heat gun is used to warm and set embossing powder. It resembles a hair dryer, but it gets much hotter.

Paper and Metal Hole Punches

One way to connect items such as paper and metal when making mixed-media jewelry is to punch holes and then use wire or jump rings to join.

Most craft and office supply stores carry different-sized holes punches, but for most metal punching, for thick plates of metal in particular, you'll need a tool specially designed for this. You can use a simple screw-type punch or, if you are more daring, a hand drill and appropriate drill bit will also do the trick.

Photo courtesy of Blick Art Materials

Paints

Select regular and metallic colors of paint to add color to wood, glass, and paper items. Most craft stores have a large paint selection, including acrylics, which are very inexpensive.

Paintbrushes

Keep a variety of fine and disposable bristle and foam brushes available for use with glues or paints. Always clean good brushes right after use.

Resins, Glazes, and Finishes

To add a finishing touch and also protect items made of materials such as paper, cover them with a clear glaze.

Resin: Resins are liquid plastics or epoxies, and can be purchased in kits. They require mixing right before use. As with all chemicals, make sure you follow manufacturers' instructions and work in well-ventilated areas. Resins are good for filling in cavities and open areas such as bottle-cap interiors. Envirotex Lite is a similar, easy-to-use reactive polymer compound that is available in craft stores.

Gel medium: Look for this in art supply stores or the art department of your local craft store. It dries clear and is useful for gluing, collage, and photo transfers.

Decoupage medium: Often used for decoupage and collage, products such as Mod Podge are useful as a sealer, adhesive, and finish. They dry clear and are available in gloss or matte finishes.

CHAPTER 2

Mixed-Media Techniques

Aside from traditional methods of construction, many of the procedures listed in this section have been borrowed from other craft forms—rubber stamping, scrapbooking, macramé, and paper arts—to name a few. This section provides a basic understanding of jewelry assembly and allows you to successfully complete the mixed-media jewelry projects in this book. When you select a project to make from this book, you'll see these same techniques in bold-faced text listed in the project instructions. This is intended as a way to cross-reference projects to the techniques described here. Just flip back to this section if you need a quick refresher.

Connections

Many jewelry items are made of components and pieces connected to each other. One piece connects to another piece and so on, until you have a finished piece of jewelry. There are several methods for connecting jewelry components but, in this book, wire is the most commonly used. The size of the wire you decide to use depends on how heavy a piece is and may also be dependant on the beads used, if any. Some general purpose wire diameters are 20 gauge for clasps (0.81 mm); 21 and 22 gauge (0.72 mm and 0.65 mm) for beaded connections; and 24 gauge (0.51 mm) for beads with narrower holes such as pearls.

Wrapped Loop

The wrapped loop technique is extremely useful for a wide variety of jewelry projects. You can use it to make earrings, add dangles to necklaces, or finish off a clasp for a bracelet. For this technique, you will need a pair of round-nosed pliers, wire cutters, flat-nosed pliers, a jeweler's file, and your choice of wire to create the wrapped loops.

1. Start by using either the flat- or round-nosed pliers to bend the wire to a 90-degree angle so that you create an upside-down L shape (**A** and **B**).

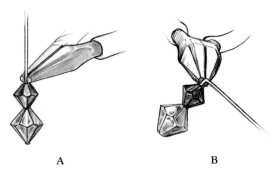

A   B

2. Position the nose of the round-nosed pliers in the bend, which you created in the previous step (**C**).

3. Use your fingers to wrap the wire around the nose of the pliers to form a loop (**D**).

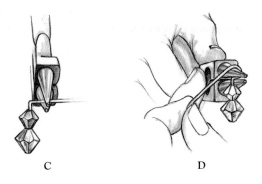

C   D

4. While keeping the round-nosed pliers inside the loop, hold the loop against the nose of the pliers

E

with one finger (**E**). You should have the round-nosed pliers in one hand with one finger pressing the loop against the nose. (If you are right-handed, use your left hand to hold the pliers and your pointer finger to hold the loop against the nose.)

5. Using your other hand (if right-handed, the right hand), start to wrap the loose wire around the straight piece of wire that is directly under the loop. If the wire is soft, you can probably do this with your fingers. Otherwise, use a bent- or flat-nosed pair of pliers to hold the loose wire and wrap (**F**).

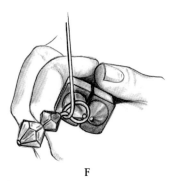

F

6. Continue to wrap as many times as you want, and if necessary, trim off excess wire and file smooth with a jeweler's file (**G**).

G

7. Use the bent-nosed pliers to press the wire-wrapped end flat to make sure it does not scratch or poke the wearer.

8. If necessary, use the round-nosed pliers to straighten the loop.

Double Loop

An alternative to the wrapped loop, the double loop technique is useful for connecting pieces that need to be closely fitted. Another advantage of this technique is that the finished double loop of wire can work much like a spring ring, so that you can attach or take apart pieces fairly easily. For this technique, you will need a pair of round-nosed pliers, wire cutters, flat-nosed pliers, jeweler's file, and your choice of wire to create wrap loops.

1. Use either the flat- or round-nosed pliers to bend the wire to a 90-degree angle so that you create an upside-down L shape (**A** and **B**).

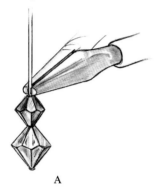

A

B

2. Position the nose of the round-nosed pliers in the bend, which you created in the previous step (**C**).

C

3. Use your fingers to wrap the wire around the nose of the pliers to form a loop (**D**).

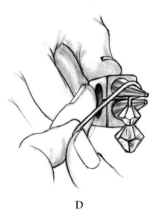

D

4. Continue to keep the nose of the pliers in the loop, and wrap the wire another time, 180 degrees around the nose of the pliers (**E**).

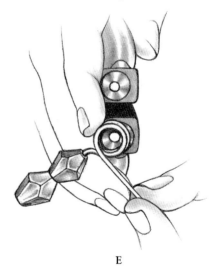

E

5. Use wire cutters to trim off excess wire, and file the ends of the wire with a jeweler's file.

Wire Wrap

*This technique is very similar to the **wrapped loop** technique, only, occasionally you will find that you need to connect two pieces of wire together without a loop on the end. For this technique, you will need at least one pair of flat- or bent-nosed pliers. If the wire is soft enough, such as 22 gauge (0.65 mm), you can hold the stationary wire with your fingers. If the wire is heavy, however, then you may need a pair of pliers in each hand for this technique.*

1. This technique requires two pieces of wire: one stationary and one working piece.

2. Hold the stationary wire with one hand, and with your other hand, use a pair of pliers to wrap the working wire around the stationary wire (**A**).

3. Once you have wrapped at least three or four times, trim off excess wire and file the end of the wire smooth with a jeweler's file (**B**).

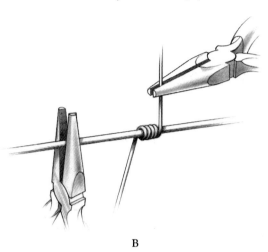

B

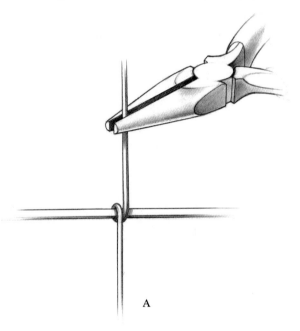

A

Simple Loop

*This technique is a simplified version of the **wrapped loop** technique and is useful for making earrings, dangles, pendants, and various other jewelry components. For this procedure, you will need a pair of round-nosed pliers, wire cutters, and a head pin. Though a head pin is being used for illustration purposes, you can also use this technique with wire.*

1. Use the round-nosed pliers to bend the head pin to a 90-degree angle (**A**).

A

2. The bent part of the head should be about ¹/₂" (1.3 cm) long. If necessary, trim excess with wire cutters.

3. Position the bent part of the head pin so that it is facing away from you.

4. Then, using round-nosed pliers, grasp the end of the bent head pin and make sure that the middle part of the pliers' nose is holding the pin. After positioning your pliers correctly, slowly curl the wire toward you (**B**).

B

5. Since the first curl will probably not complete the circle yet, release and reposition the pliers on the circle you have started.

6. Continue to curl it toward you until you have made a circle (**C**).

C

Basic Hook

Learning to make your own hook out of wire is a wonderful bit of freedom from the prefabricated jewelry components on the market. It is great to be able to make your own hook when you need it and not have to worry about running down to the bead shop or placing an order and waiting for your jewelry supplies to arrive. It also adds a little hand-crafted touch to the finished pieces. For this technique, you will need round-nosed pliers and a jeweler's file.

1. After filing the ends of the wire, take the round-nosed pliers and make a loop or curl on one end of the wire (**A**).

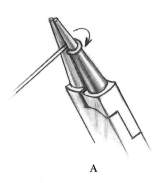

A

2. Now, measuring approximately ¹/₂" (1.3 cm) from the end of the curl, grasp the wire with the round-nosed pliers, using the middle part of the pliers' nose.

3. Holding the pliers with one hand, use your other hand to wrap the wire around the nose of your pliers to create a hook shape (**B**).

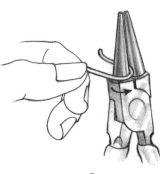

B

4. Using the round-nosed pliers, create a tiny curl on the end of the hook you created in the previous step (**C**).

C

Basic Eye

By using a little wire, you can fashion this simple figure-eight design. The two loops on this piece combine to work as the second part of a clasp, which is made to team up with any number of hook-style clasps. To make a figure-eight eye, you will need approximately 1¹/₂" (3.8 cm) of wire, a jeweler's file, and round-nosed pliers.

1. Use a jeweler's file to smooth both ends of the wire.

2. Use the round-nosed pliers to make a large loop on one end of the wire so that you have used up half of the piece of wire (**A**).

A

3. Do the same with the other end of the wire, but this time the loop should be facing the other direction so that you make a figure eight with the wire (**B**).

B

"S" Hook

The "S" design is a very versatile wire shape that can be used for all kinds of components. It works as a clasp or as other jewelry components, depending on the design of the jewelry piece. All you need is about 2" (5.1 cm) of wire, a jeweler's file, and round-nosed pliers.

1. Use a jeweler's file to smooth the ends of your wire.

2. Place the nose of the round-nosed pliers a little higher than halfway down the wire, and curl one end of the wire around the nose to create a hook shape (**A**).

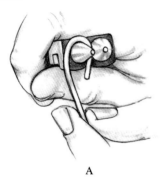

A

3. Repeat this on the other end of the wire so that the hook is facing the opposite direction (**B**).

B

4. Again, use round-nosed pliers to make the smallest possible curls on both ends of your wire hook (**C**).

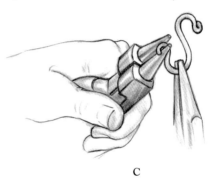

C

Open and Close Jump Rings

Jump rings are a great way to connect jewelry parts. Many jewelry suppliers sell prefabricated jump rings that are already sized and cut, ready to use. It is very important to open and close jump rings properly or you can damage the integrity of the piece. Also, make sure you purchase quality jump rings that are precisely cut. For both opening and closing jump rings, you'll need two pairs of pliers, one for each hand.

1. To close a jump ring, start with a pair of pliers in each hand, and grasp both sides of the ring on either side of the cut area (**A**).

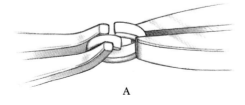

A

2. Simultaneously close the ring by moving one hand away from you and the other towards you until both sides meet (**B**).

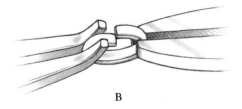

B

3. When the two sides meet, you should hear a snapping sound, indicating that both sides are flush (**C**).

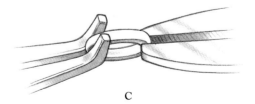

C

4. To open a jump ring, repeat the same process using two pairs of pliers in both hands, simultaneously moving one toward you and one away.

Snake Wire Components

*This component is very similar to the **"S" hook**; it's just more exaggerated. You will need about 6" (15.2 cm) of wire, round-nosed pliers, wire cutters, and a jeweler's file. A hammer and bench block are optional if you want to flatten areas of the snake after you make it.*

1. With round-nosed pliers, make a curl on one end of the wire (**A**).

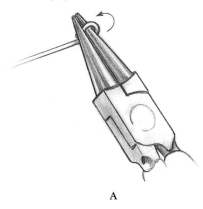

A

2. Again, using round-nosed pliers, hold the wire piece just past the curl previously made, and bend the wire 90 degrees (**B**).

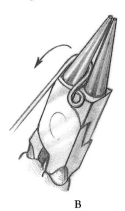

B

3. About ½" (1.3 cm) from the bent area, hold the wire again with pliers and wrap another 90 degrees in the opposite direction as before (at this point you should start to recognize the snake form) (**C**).

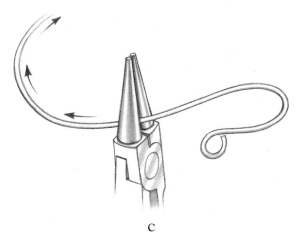

C

4. Repeat the above step, only this time place the pliers about 1" (2.5 cm) down on the wire.

5. Repeat step 3, make another small curl, trim off excess wire, file, and bend the curl straight up so that it matches the other end of the wire snake (**C**).

Metal Eyelets

This technique is a good example of the crossover that is available to mixed-media jewelry artists if you are already familiar with other types of crafting. Eyelets have been used for a long time in scrapbook and other paper arts as embellishments and ways to connect pieces together, most often paper pieces. Eyelets come in many different sizes, so the different-sized holes for each eyelet can add to the overall design of the finished piece and at the same time function as a place to connect earrings hooks or clasps. To make eyelets, you'll need a hard surface to work on, a small metal hammer, hole punch, metal eyelets, and an eyelet setter. You need a setter and hole punch that are the same size of your eyelets. See page 10 for more on eyelet setting kits.

1. Determine where you want your eyelet to be placed, and use a hole punch to punch a hole in this spot.

2. Put the eyelet in the hole with the back of the eyelet (the side that is not flat) facing you (**A**).

3. Position the setter in the middle of the eyelet, and hit the end of the setter firmly with the hammer. You may have to do this a few times to ensure the eyelet is flattened (**B**).

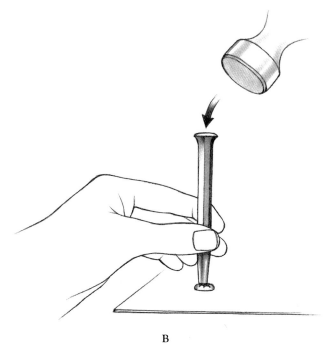

B

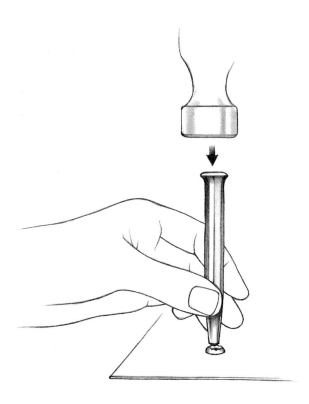

A

Crimp Beads

A beaded piece of jewelry can be finished on the ends with crimp beads. In order to use this method, you will need a pair of crimping pliers and crimp beads (I highly recommend using tube-shaped crimp beads because they are easy to work with), round-nosed pliers, wire cutters, and beading wire.

1. Slide one crimp bead onto the end of a piece of beading wire, and loop the wire back through the crimp bead (**A**).

A

2. Position the crimp bead inside the second notch in the crimping pliers (the one closest to you when you are holding the pliers in your hand), and close the pliers around the bead. You should see the crimp bead now has a groove down the middle so that it curls (**B**).

B

3. Position the same crimp bead in the first notch in the pliers, and close the pliers around it so that you are flattening the curl (**C** and **D**).

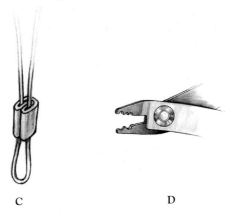

C   D

4. Use wire cutters to trim off all but about 1/4" (6 mm) of excess beading wire.

5. Add your beads, making sure to slide the first bead over both pieces of wire on the end.

6. Once you have all of your beads on, you are ready to finish the other end. Slide a second crimp bead onto the end of the wire so it comes after the last bead strung.

7. Loop the wire back through the crimp bead as well as the last bead of the piece.

8. Insert the nose of the round-nosed pliers into the loop.

9. While holding your round-nosed pliers with one hand, gently pull the beading wire with your other hand so that you push the crimp bead snug against the other beads. This will ensure that you do not have any extra slack in your beaded piece and that you also keep the end loop of your beading wire intact.

10. Repeat steps 2 and 3 above to close the crimp bead.

11. Use wire cutters to carefully trim off excess beading wire.

Surface Treatments

There are lots of different ways to approach decorating or protecting the surface of your mixed-media jewelry, but this section covers a few of the more popular methods.

Collage

Layering paper pieces and found objects is a wonderful way to add depth and unique treatments to your finished piece of jewelry. There are no specific rules on how to collage, but the idea is to layer and arrange items in unexpected, free-form designs. Adhere the items together with glue or finishing media such as gel medium or Mod Podge, which also act as a sealer. In addition, you need a foam brush and your choice of decorative elements such as pretty papers, tissue, watch parts, or postage stamps. Look for small items that are easy to glue and layer onto a flat surface.

1. Once you have a plan for your collage, start by coating the backs of the collage items and arranging them on the surface of the jewelry you are decorating.

2. Allow to dry, and add more layers if desired.

3. Add a few topcoats, allowing each to dry in between applications, to create a protective layer over the finished piece.

Stamping

When selecting stamps, consider how you will use the end product. Most stamp manufacturers will include their copyright policies either directly on the packaging or website, so make sure you are aware of these. Normally, this isn't an issue if you plan to make items and give them away, but if you want to sell a piece of jewelry at a later date, then look for stamp companies that offer stamps with what is referred to an "angel policy." This means they usually allow you to sell a small number of hand-stamped items using their stamped images. Once you have the right stamp, baby wipes (which are great for cleaning your stamps right after use), and your ink pad, you can get started.

1. Begin by inking your stamp. Hold the stamp against the ink pad, using even pressure (**A**).

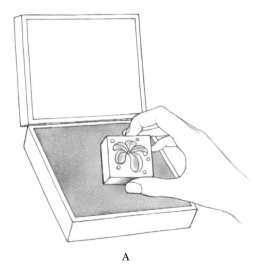

A

2. Firmly press the inked stamp onto the surface you want to decorate, and then lift up. Do not rock the stamp back and forth while stamping as this can create doubled images (**B**).

B

3. Once you get the basics of stamping, consider branching out into embossing. This will give the stamped image a raised effect, and requires pigment or embossing ink, embossing powder, and a heat gun.

Knotting

Used for connecting, sectioning off, and finishing off different areas on a piece of jewelry, knots are easy but still important methods to master.

Overhand Knot

You probably already know how to make an overhand knot, but here is a quick refresher. It is useful for knotting ends, knotting between beads, or attaching jewelry components together and works well with leather, ribbon, yarns, and nylon cord.

1. Make a loop with the stringing medium (**A**).

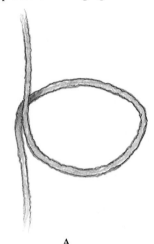

A

2. Bring one end of the cord under and through the loop (**B**).

3. Pull both ends of the string to tighten the knot (**C**).

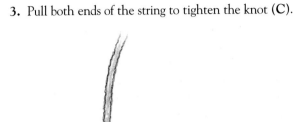

B

C

Knot with Bead

Knotting between beads is a way to incorporate the stringing medium—ribbon, colored beading wire, leather, or nylon—and secure the beads in place. This method provides a way to create a station of beads along the stringing medium of choice. It also allows for a nice draping effect. To knot between beads, you need a corsage pin (serious bead stringers may already have a beading awl for this, which works fine as well), your choice of stringing medium and beads, and of course, the best tools you have—your fingers.

1. Tie a loose overhand knot (**A**).

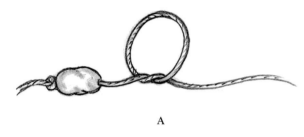

A

2. Insert the corsage pin through the loose knot (**B**).

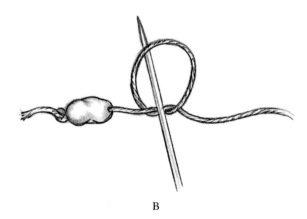

B

3. Use one hand to push the pin and knot down toward the bead, and hold the cord with your other hand until the pin and knot are flush against the bead (**C**).

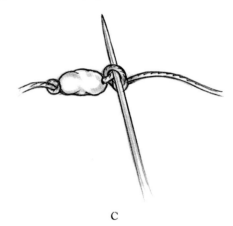

C

4. Keeping the knot up against the bead, carefully slip the end of the pin out of the knot and immediately use your fingers to push the knot against the bead.

Mounting Knot

Mature macramé jewelry artists will remember this knot. It is normally used to attach one cord to another, but it is useful for attaching cord to a number of other objects such as pendants, beads, or charms.

1. Fold the cord in half, and locate the middle area where the cord is folded.

2. Holding the folded area of the cord together, insert it through the hole in a jewelry component you want to attach. This will make a loop (**A**).

3. Slip the ends of the rest of the cord through this loop, and pull the ends to anchor the cord to the component (**B**).

B

A

Square Knot

The traditional square knot is one of the strongest and easiest knotting techniques. The average person probably already knows how to do this, though she may not know the knot by name. It is most often used for finishing off a beaded piece of jewelry such as a bracelet or necklace.

1. Position the ends of the cord in the shape of an X so that the right end is over the left end of the cord.

2. Bring the right cord over and under the other end of the cord, and pull both ends tightly so that you have the first part of the knot completed (**A**).

3. Repeat step 1, but instead position the left end over the right end of the cord.

4. Bring the left cord over and under the other end of the cord, and pull both ends tightly to complete the square knot (**B**).

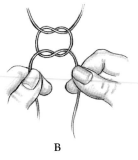

B

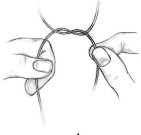

A

CHAPTER 3

Ephemera and Memory

Categorizing mixed-media jewelry is difficult. It feels like forcing a square peg into a round hole because there is really no one method or one medium that defines a particular style. Mixed-media artwork does not force the artist into one genre but instead encourages experimentation. However, because some organizational methodology is necessary, I've divided the jewelry into three types: Ephemera and Memory, Collectibles and Souvenirs, and Found Objects and Natural Materials.

Like a dream that seems so real when you are asleep but is a hazy memory a few hours after awakening, ephemeral materials don't last forever. But the memories can be preserved, especially if they are memorialized in a lovely piece of jewelry. The Ephemera and Memory category includes such materials as paper scraps, photos, lace, or ribbon. Photographs can fade over time, and fabric will someday unravel. But, just because they don't last forever doesn't mean you can't use ephemeral materials to make wonderful mixed-media jewelry. Just as other media such as scrapbooking and altered books have incorporated decorative papers, stamping methods, fibers, and collage, these materials and techniques can also be applied to jewelry making.

Designer's Tip

Note: As you read through the project instructions, you will also see references, identified with bold text, to the techniques outlined in the Mixed-Media Techniques section of this book. Refer to that section as needed to complete the projects.

Shoe Queen Necklace

What woman doesn't occasionally drool over a pair of Pradas or Jimmy Choos? Mixed-media artist Victoria Button shows off her love of footwear in this "kicky" necklace. Even if you don't worship shoes (maybe your obsession is purses or jewelry), you can use this piece to declare your own fashion passion. Just cut a few fun words or images from a magazine or even some junk mail, and lacquer them onto a shell bead to make your tiny billboard. Some basic wire work allows you to make a curly sterling bale that frames the bead. Attach some sterling chain, embellish with more wire and beads, and you are good to go shopping.

MATERIALS

- small paper images (from magazines, books, stickers, etc.)
- one 2$\frac{1}{2}$ mm square-shaped Paua shell bead
- 2" (5.1 cm) 24-gauge (0.51 mm) sterling head pin
- 12" (30.5 cm) 24-gauge (0.51 mm) sterling round wire
- three 5 mm white pearl beads
- two 4 mm faceted moss agate beads
- two 6 mm rondelle coral beads
- three 5 mm sterling jump rings
- one 5 mm sterling lobster-claw clasp with attached ring
- 20" (50.8 cm) fine-link chain
- Mod Podge (gloss finish)
- foam brush
- round-nosed pliers
- flat-nosed pliers
- wire cutters
- scissors

Designer's Tip

Believe it or not, Emily Dickinson kept a file of clippings, which she used to embellish her poems and letters to friends and relatives. Start your own personal clippings file with bits and pieces you come across that "speak to you." If you don't subscribe to many magazines, consider making a trip to your local library. Many libraries discard (yes, actually throw out) old or damaged books and magazines. Check their sales racks, but also ask the librarian behind the desk if they have any old books or magazines that they plan to throw out. You may find your own personal gold mine of clip art.

(continued from page 28)

INSTRUCTIONS

1. Select a few paper images for your pin. You can use purchased stickers or clip images from catalogs, magazines, or old books.

2. Using the **collage** technique and Mod Podge, decorate the shell bead.

3. After the bead is dry, paint five more layers of Mod Podge onto the bead, allowing each layer to dry before adding the next.

4. While the bead is drying, start assembling the chain part of the necklace. Use wire cutters to cut off a 5" (12.7 cm) piece of chain.

5. Use flat-nosed pliers to slightly open the ring on the lobster-claw clasps. Slip the end of the chain onto the ring and close the ring. (If you can't find a clasp with a ring already attached, just add your own jump ring to the clasp.)

6. With sterling wire, make a **wrapped loop**. Before closing the loop, attach the other end of the chain piece to the loop.

7. Thread one agate bead, one coral bead, and one pearl bead onto the wire, and begin another **wrapped loop** on the wire, but do not close the loop yet.

8. Cut 3" (7.6 cm) of chain. Slip one end onto the loop made in the previous step, then wrap the loop closed. Set this part of the necklace aside for later use.

9. Cut two 2" (5.1 cm) pieces of chain.

10. Thread one pearl bead onto the head pin. Begin making a **wrapped loop** on the head pin and, before closing the loop, secure one end of the one piece of chain onto the loop.

11. Open a jump ring, slip on the other end of the chain with the pearl dangle created in the previous step, and pick up the other chain piece cut in step 9. Attach this also to the jump ring before closing the jump ring.

12. Cut a 5" (12.7 cm) piece of chain, and attach this using another jump ring to the end of the chain from the previous step.

13. Repeat steps 6 through 8 for the rest of the chain piece, then set aside for later use.

14. Take about 5" (12.7 cm) of wire, and, using round-nosed pliers, curl one end of the wire.

15. Insert the other end of the wire through the shell bead (which should be completely dry at this point), and again, with round-nosed pliers, make an equal-size curl on the other end of the wire.

16. With your fingers, position the wire so that there is an equal amount of wire on either side of the bead, then bend the wire so that the curls cover the top corners on both sides of the bead. You may need to curl the wire a little more or fiddle with it to get it positioned how you want it, but the wire is soft and should be easy to bend with your fingers.

17. Once the wire is positioned, add five more layers of Mod Podge, letting each coat dry before adding the next. Cover both the wire and the bead with the Mod Podge to help keep the wire secured to the bead.

18. To complete the necklace, use jump rings to attach the chain segments of the necklace to the curls of wire on the bead.

Pink Paper Paradise Earrings

The combination of paper, rubber, and metal is unusual, but it works in these festive and colorful earrings designed by the team of Elizabeth Glass Geltman and her daughter Rachel Geltman. The rubber for these earrings was rescued from the garbage, but you can find thin rubber sheeting at most hardware stores. Pink or any other color is an option for the paper pieces that are sandwiched in between. The paper pieces do not need to be cut exactly, nor do the rubber pieces. The mixed sizes create the fun, irregular dimensions. Again, the hardware store is a reliable place to find copper wire, but most wire jewelry suppliers also carry copper.

MATERIALS

- four pieces of text-weight paper
- four pieces of $1/8$" (3 mm)-thick $3/4$" × $3/4$" (1.9 × 1.9 cm) rubber squares
- 20" (50.8 cm) 20-gauge (0.81 mm) copper wire
- four 24 mm domed copper discs
- embroidery needle
- round-nosed pliers
- flat-nosed pliers
- flush cutter
- jeweler's file
- scissors
- ruler
- pencil

(continued from page 31)

INSTRUCTIONS

1. Cut the paper until you have 128 squares $3/4" \times 3/4"$ (1.9 × 1.9 cm), and separate them into two equal stacks. The pieces do not have to be cut exactly since they will spin a little when the earrings are assembled.

2. Use an embroidery needle to punch holes in the middle of all the paper squares.

3. Repeat this for the rubber pieces, puncturing the center of each piece with the needle.

4. Taking about 10" (25.4 cm) of copper wire, use round-nosed pliers to form a hook on one end of the wire.

5. Measure down about $1/2"$ (1.3 cm) from the hook, and use flat-nosed pliers to bend the wire at a 90-degree angle.

6. Thread on one copper dome (curved side facing away from the wrapped loop), one piece of rubber, one stack of paper, another piece of rubber, and a second copper dome (facing opposite the first dome), creating a sandwich with the materials.

7. Hold the pencil vertically against the wire that is sticking out of the top of the dome, and wrap the wire around the pencil three times.

8. Measure down on the remaining wire about 1" (2.5 cm), hold the pencil horizontally against the wire, and bend the wire 180 degrees around the pencil.

9. Measure down about 2" (5.1 cm) on the wire, and use round-nosed pliers to slightly bend the end of the wire.

10. Cut any remaining wire, and file as necessary to smooth.

11. Repeat steps 4 through 10 for the other earring.

Designer's Tip

If you want to be a little more daring, instead of purchasing the domed copper sections for the Pink Paper Paradise Earrings, you can make them yourself using basic metal fabrication tools. Use a saw to cut out copper circles and a hand drill or drill press to punch holes through the copper discs. To form the circles into half-dome shapes, you need a doming block, daps, and a hammer. (A doming block is a block of metal that has a dome-shaped dip in it, and daps are metal stakes used with a hammer to punch the copper into the doming block.) For the half-circles used in these earrings, simply place the copper pieces over the dip in the block, position a dap on it, and strike with a hammer.

Bricolage Pendant

With the help of decorative papers and a little imagination, artist Pam Sanders transforms simple card stock and mat board into a collage pendant that looks as if it was dug up from the ruins of an ancient civilization. Along with collage techniques, wire helps to create a frame for the finished pendant. Copper wire is excellent to use on a piece that you want to eventually have an aged look because eventually oxidation will darken the metal for a patina effect. Waxed linen fiber adorned with a few beads completes the strap.

MATERIALS

- two 2" × 4" (5.1 × 10.2 cm) pieces of card stock
- two 2" × 2" (5.1 × 5.1 cm) pieces of mat board
- two 2" × 4" (5.1 × 10.2 cm) pieces of black handmade paper
- your choice of decorative papers (one with face, one with words, one with pattern)
- scraps of tissue paper
- 20" (50.8 cm) 24-gauge (0.51 mm) copper wire
- 72" (182.9 cm) 20-gauge (0.81 mm) copper wire
- three turquoise nugget beads
- three copper-colored glass bugle beads
- three copper-colored glass triangle beads
- eleven 4 mm jasper rondelle beads
- four 4 mm copper daisy spacer beads
- four 4 mm matte beads
- seven 4 mm amber-colored beads
- two 6 mm copper-colored glass beads
- three 2" (5.1 cm) decorative head pins
- decoupage medium
- rubber stamp of words
- black ink stamp pad
- acrylic spray sealer
- 48" (121.9 cm) waxed linen cord
- bamboo skewer
- scissors
- foam brush
- wire cutters
- round-nosed pliers
- jeweler's file
- bench block
- chasing hammer

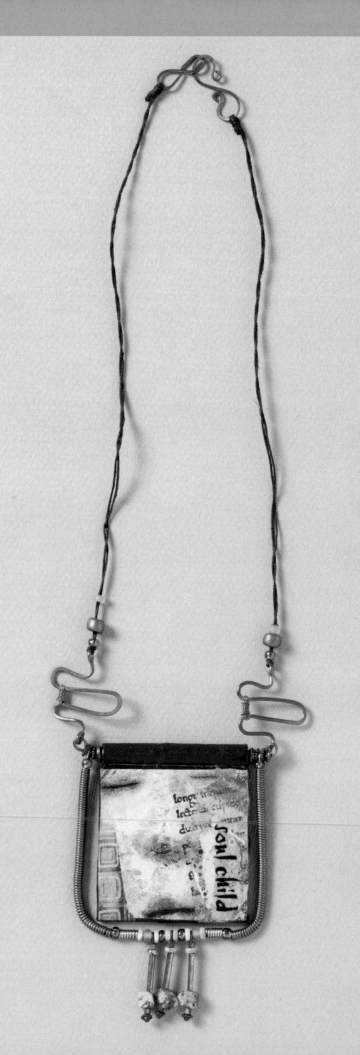

(continued from page 34)

INSTRUCTIONS

1. Make a paper bead by rolling one piece of card stock around the skewer, and use decoupage medium to glue the seams of the paper so that one overlaps the other. Let the bead dry.

2. Pull the skewer out of the paper bead made in the previous step, and glue the paper bead in the middle of the other piece of card stock. Let the glue dry.

3. Fold the flat card stock piece in half so that it encircles the paper bead.

4. Glue mat board to one side of the folded card stock piece, making sure the paper bead is at the top of the board piece. Repeat this, gluing the other mat board piece to the other side of the folded card stock. The result is a sandwich where the flat card stock pieces are secured in between two mat board pieces, and the paper bead is positioned at the top of this entire piece.

5. Using **collage**, cover both sides of the mat board with black paper pieces. Let the pendant dry.

6. Add your choice of decorative papers wherever you wish, again using **collage**.

7. After the papers are dry, use your choice of rubber stamp(s) with words and a black ink pad to stamp over the papers. (Refer to **stamping** for tips.)

8. Let the ink dry, and spray the front and back with a coat of acrylic sealer. Let the sealer dry completely before adding the wire and strap.

9. Take one head pin, thread on one triangle bead, one turquoise bead, one bugle bead, one jasper bead, and one triangle bead, and make a **simple loop** at the top. Repeat this for two more head pin pieces and set these all aside for later use.

10. Make a long coil of wire by wrapping approximately 36" (91.4 cm) of 20-gauge (0.81 mm) wire around the bamboo skewer. After coiling, the piece should be approximately 20" (50.8 cm) in length.

11. With wire cutters, cut off two 1/2" (1.3 cm) sections of coil and two 2 1/2" (6.4 cm) sections of coil. Set these aside for later use.

12. Cut a 3 1/4" (8.3 cm) piece of 20-gauge (0.81 mm) wire, and form the piece into a large U shape so that it frames the outside of the pendant.

13. Onto this U-shaped wire, thread one jasper bead, one matte bead, one head pin piece (from step 9), one jasper bead, one amber-colored bead, one jasper bead, one head pin piece, one jasper bead, one amber-colored bead, one jasper bead, one head pin piece (this will be the third head pin), one matte bead, and one jasper bead.

14. Thread on one 1/2" (1.3 cm) piece of wire coil (from step 11), one amber-colored bead, one piece of 2 1/2" (6.4 cm) piece of wire (from step 11), and one amber-colored bead.

15. Make a **simple loop** at the end of the U-shaped piece after the last amber bead.

16. Repeat steps 14 and 15 for the other side of the U-shaped wire piece.

17. Cut a 3" (7.6 cm) piece of 20-gauge (0.81 mm) wire. Using round-nosed pliers, make a small curl on the end.

18. Thread onto the wire one daisy spacer, one loop from the U-shaped wire piece previously created, one daisy spacer, and one copper rondelle.

19. Thread the copper wire through the decoupage pendant previously created. On the end of the wire, thread on one copper rondelle, one daisy spacer, the second loop on the U-shaped wire piece, and one daisy spacer.

20. Use round-nosed pliers to make another loop on the end of the wire in order to secure all the pieces—U-shaped wire piece, decoupage pendant, and beads.

21. Following the **snake wire component** technique, use two pieces of 20-gauge (0.81 mm) wire, each 3" (7.6 cm) long, and make two **snake wire components**.

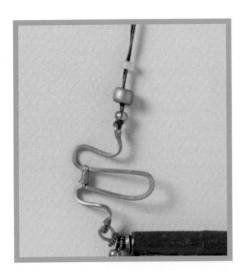

22. Set the snake wire pieces on a bench block, and lightly hammer the curved areas, not the looped sections, of the snake using a chasing hammer. This optional step will flatten the wire in the center area of the snake.

23. Cut two pieces of 24-gauge (0.51 mm) wire, each 10" (25.4 cm) long.

24. Connect one piece of wire to the middle part of the snake with **wrapped loops**, and then wrap the wire around itself from bottom to top.

25. Repeat this with the other piece of 10" (25.4 cm) wire, trim off excess wire, and file with a jeweler's file as necessary.

26. Attach the **simple loops** on both snake wire pieces to both ends of the pendant previously created.

27. Take 24" (61 cm) of waxed linen cord, fold it in half, and use a **mounting knot** to secure it to one loop of a snake piece.

28. Onto the doubled linen cord, thread one amber-colored bead, one 6 mm copper-colored bead, and one matte bead.

29. Make a **basic eye** and an **"S" hook** with copper wire. Again, hammer flat with a bench block and chasing hammer if you want to flatten the wire.

30. Take the doubled linen cord and use a **square knot** to tie it to one side of the clasp. Use scissors to trim off excess cord. Repeat this for the other side of the necklace to complete.

Mischief-Maker Earrings

Create mischief with these easy-to-make paper earrings. Mixed-media artist Linda O'Brien combines paper supplies and even some office products in these edgy earrings that only require a little paper, a smidgen of gold leaf, and a few inches of wire. Look for vintage images in old books and postcards, then photocopy or scan them in so you can use them repeatedly. Paper can be a challenge to use with jewelry designs as it is a porous material, but by covering it in self-adhesive laminate, available at most office supply stores, you can protect your tiny piece of artwork.

MATERIALS

- card stock
- gold leaf
- green and gold acrylic paint
- paintbrush
- water
- paper plate
- copies of vintage images trimmed to size
- computer-generated text
- choice of colored pencil
- matte medium
- gold leaf
- two $1/16$" (1.6 mm) copper eyelets
- $1/16$" (1.6 mm) hole punch
- eyelet setter
- small metal hammer
- two 4" (10.2 cm) pieces of 20-gauge (0.81 mm) sterling wire
- two sterling ear hooks
- scissors
- ruler
- self-adhesive laminate sheet

(continued from page 38)

INSTRUCTIONS

1. Cut card stock into two pieces, each 1" × 1¹/₈" (2.5 × 2.9 cm).

2. Squeeze the paints onto a paper plate, and add few drops of water to thin the paints.

3. Paint one side of the paper pieces, let dry, and then repeat on the other side. Make sure both pieces of paper are completely dry.

4. Take a small amount of gold leaf and using the end of the paintbrush, burnish a few dots of gold leaf onto a few areas on what will be the front of the paper earrings.

5. Adhere the trimmed images to both pieces of paper using matte medium.

6. Cut out the computer-generated text, color around it using a colored pencil, and adhere it to the paper. On one earring, adhere the word *mischief* and to the other earring, adhere the word *maker*.

7. Insert both pieces into the self-adhesive laminate, follow the manufacturer's instructions to seal the laminate, and trim away excess.

8. Use the **eyelet** technique to add eyelets to the top of each earring piece.

9. With sterling wire, use the **wrapped loop** technique to make a looped wire piece on each earring. Instead of trimming off extra wire, continue to wrap it around the looped area to create extra wraps. Don't worry about being too neat. A little unevenness adds character.

10. Attach the ear hooks to the top of the sterling loops on both earrings.

Designer's Tip

When first learning how to make jewelry, it is important to follow the rules and materials list as best you can. Obviously, if you don't use the same instructions, tools, and supplies, you won't achieve the same results. However, once you get a few basics down, there's no reason not to add a little trademark of your own by breaking the rules. Perfectly wrapped loops look nice and professional, but by adding extra wraps to a jewelry piece, you can add character and whimsy to the finished design.

Perfect Metal Pins

Start with a little paper crafting, add a dash of fiber wrapping, and mix in a little scrapbooking and you get these faux metal pins designed by Julia Andrus. The base is made with card stock, and the embellishments include: miniature brads, the kind used to connect paper pieces in scrapbooks; scraps of fibers, such as yarns and metallic threads; glass marbles, commonly used in floral design work; tiny images, the same size as the marbles; and metallic paints and patinas, to use as you please. Once you learn the basics of this design, you'll want to make lots of them to wear and give out as tiny gifts of wearable artwork.

MATERIALS

- two 1³/₄" (4.4 cm) black card stock squares
- one 1" (2.5 cm) black card stock square
- metallic or patina powdered pigments (such as Perfect Pearls)
- resin-based medium (such as Perfect Medium)
- glue stick
- three square metal-colored mini-brads
- one 16 mm glass floral marble
- one 16 mm paper image
- fiber or ribbon
- pin back
- fine-grit sandpaper
- adhesive
- small round-hole punch
- small square-hole punch
- pencil
- plastic bowl
- paintbrush
- paper towels

Designer's Tip

Keep a small bag, pouch, or tin to collect and store fiber scraps. Lace, metallic threads, yarns, ribbon, and small fabric swatches may seem like items to throw away, but eventually, when you have enough saved, they can be used as single embellishments or merged together to make small fiber artwork that you can wear. To help your fiber scrap collection grow, get the word out to friends and family and ask them to save any bits and pieces to be donated to the cause. Children's discarded hair ribbons or leftovers from an amateur seamstress can quickly expand your collection.

(continued from page 41)

INSTRUCTIONS

1. Take one piece of 1³/₄" (4.4 cm) card stock, and, using a pencil, mark three spots on the left side where the brads will go later. Also mark spots on either side of the bottom of the card stock for the future notches.

2. Use a round-hole punch and then a square-hole punch to punch out the brad spots and the notches, and then use this same piece of card stock as a template to cut the same areas out of the other piece of 1³/₄" (4.4 cm) card stock.

3. Layer and glue the squares together, making sure the holes are aligned.

4. Use sandpaper to smooth and sand the edges of the glued card stock.

5. In a plastic bowl, mix powdered pigments with water to form a creamy paint.

6. Brush the mixed pigment paint over the glued card stock piece and immediately buff off with a paper towel for a satin finish. For a more polished finish, paint in both directions and let dry for a few seconds.

7. If you want to make the paper look like pounded metal, pound the handle end of the paintbrush against the paper piece. Sand the edges for more distressing.

8. Take the 1" (2.5 cm) piece of card stock, and rub the surface with a resin-based medium then dust with your choice of pigment paints. For a distressed and rusty look, dampen the brush and stipple, dabbing the bristles against the paint with more patina colored pigment paint.

9. Once all the paint is dried, glue the small square on top of the bigger square previously prepared.

10. Glue a pin back to the back of the paper pieces and allow to dry.

11. Cut out the paper image, making sure it is the same size as the bottom of the glass marble. Glue the image to the marble, and then glue the marble to the small square.

12. Wrap and tie your choice of fibers around the notches in the bottom of the pin, and add the brads to the three holes on the side to complete.

Paper Faux-Enamel Set

This jewelry set flaunts the look of bold and beautiful enamel, yet only you will know it is light as a feather when you wear it. Learn the paint and paper tricks revealed to you by designer Julia Andrus in these faux enamel earrings and matching multistrand necklace. Besides the fashionable appeal of the finished product, the kicker is that many of the materials used for this project are readily available from craft stores and websites. You may even have some card stock in your craft stash that is waiting to turn into faux enamel jewelry pieces.

MATERIALS

- black card stock
- powdered pigments in gold, patina blue, patina green, and copper (such as Perfect Pearls)
- resin-based medium (such as Perfect Medium)
- clear embossing enamel (such as Ultra Thick Embossing Enamel)
- 36" (91.4 cm) 20-gauge (0.81 mm) brass wire
- 18" (45.7 cm) brown satin cord
- 17" (43.2 cm) brown satin cord
- 16" (40.6 cm) brown satin cord
- glue stick
- clear finishing spray (gloss finish)
- heat gun
- 17 mm circle punch or die cut
- 12 mm circle punch or die cut
- small hole punch
- mixing tray and paintbrushes
- fine-grit sandpaper
- round-nosed pliers
- flat-nosed pliers
- wire cutters
- 10 mm sterling toggle clasp
- 10 mm sterling pinch end
- earring posts with dangle and clutch
- assorted 4 mm glass beads (blue, copper, gold, and amber)
- scissors
- waxed paper
- plastic knife
- ruler

(continued from page 44)

INSTRUCTIONS

1. Punch out four discs of black card stock 17 mm in diameter.

2. With the glue stick, glue these together, then use a small hole punch to punch a hole in the top. Lightly sand the edges.

3. Repeat steps 1 and 2 until you have a total of thirteen discs 17 mm in diameter.

4. Repeat steps 1 and 2, except use a 12 mm punch or die cut. Repeat until you have a total of eleven smaller discs.

5. After all the glue is dry, arrange the paper pieces on a sheet of waxed paper.

6. Mix the pigment powders with a little water, and paint the edges and one side of each paper piece.

7. Once the paint is dry, repeat the painting process on the other side of each piece. Let dry again.

8. Apply resin-based medium to one side of a paper piece, sprinkle with embossing enamel, and use a heat gun to heat until melted and glossy. Repeat the embossing process on the other side.

9. Repeat step 8 for all the paper pieces.

10. Brush the correlating color of dry pigment over each piece (gold, blue, green, or copper). The resins in the pigment powders and embossing enamel will bind and make a glossy metallic finish.

11. Spray all pieces with clear glossy finish on one side, dry, and repeat on the other side. Let dry before continuing.

12. Cut out six rectangular pieces of card stock, each 1" × 1½" (2.5 × 3.8 cm), then glue three of the six together.

13. Layer and glue the other three rectangles together.

14. Take 2" (5.1 cm) of wire, and use round-nosed pliers to bend into a small U shape. Glue the wire piece in between the two squares so that the U shape is sticking out to form a small bale. Sand the edges and let dry.

15. Apply a solid coat of pigment paint to paint the back of the rectangle. Paint the front with all four colors (gold, blue, green, and copper), and let dry.

16. Pat the front of the rectangle with resin-based medium, sprinkle on embossing enamel, and heat.

17. During the heating process, sprinkle on more embossing enamel to build up the thickness and continue to heat until glossy.

18. When cool, pat with more resin-based medium, apply some pigment powder, sprinkle with embossing enamel, and heat again. This time, start at a distance so the powder won't blow away, then slowly move closer as it becomes tacky.

19. Turn off the heat gun and immediately rake a plastic knife over the piece to create texture. Depending on how molten the embossing enamel is, you may need to wait a few seconds before raking.

20. Rub with some pigment powder in spots to create highlights, and spray with a gloss finish.

21. Once you have prepared all the discs and rectangle, you are ready to assemble the earrings and necklace. For the earrings, take a few inches of wire, make a **simple loop**, and attach one small and then one large disc onto the loop so that the smaller disc is on top of the larger disc.

22. Thread one or two glass beads onto the wire, make another **simple loop** at the top of the wire, and attach this to the earring post loop.

23. Repeat steps 21 and 22 for the second ear-ring, making sure to use the same colored discs and beads so they match.

24. For the necklace, use the longest cord for the rectangular section. Use a **mounting knot** to attach the center of the cord to the rectangular bale.

25. Hold the two sides of the cord together and tie an **overhand knot**.

26. Separate the cords and, measuring about 1/2" (1.3 cm) down on one cord, tie another **overhand knot**.

27. Repeat step 26, measuring and knotting down both sides of the cord until you have three **overhand knots** on both sides.

28. Take a few inches of wire, make a **simple loop**, and attach one small disc onto the loop.

29. Thread one or two glass beads, make another **simple loop** at the top of the wire, and attach this to the area or cord in between the knots.

30. Repeat steps 28 and 29, making alternate dangles of large and small discs. Attach to the cord until you have one small, one large, and one small disc on one side of the cord, and the same disc pattern (small, large, small) on the other side of the cord.

31. For the second longest cord, repeat steps 26 through 30, spacing out the **overhand knots** on the cord and adding seven disc dangles in this order: two large, one small, one large, one small, and two large.

32. To make the final strand (and the shortest of the three), again add seven disc dangles, but this time they should alternate: one large, one small, and so on, ending with one large.

33. Graduate the cord lengths for assembly by putting the longest cord (the one with the rectangle) first, then the 17" (43.2 cm), and then the 16" (40.6 cm) cords together.

Designer's Tip

When using alternative beading media like satin cords, organza, or velvet, look for alternative ways to finish them and attach a clasp. Fiber is more popular than ever for jewelry making, so many jewelry making suppliers sell specialty components designed for finish fibers to help incorporate them into jewelry. Some of these include pinch ends, metal cones, coil crimps, and crimp ends. Make sure to use a sharp pair of scissors to cut fibers before ending, and if you are concerned with fraying, try to coat the ends with either a little clear drying glue or a product such as Stop Fray.

34. Trim off excess cord, insert the ends of the cords into the sterling pinch end, and use flat-nosed pliers to close the pinch end around the cord.

35. Repeat this for the other side of the cords, and attach a toggle clasp to both sides of the necklace. (Many toggle clasps come with jump rings attached, but if yours doesn't, you'll need two extra 5 mm jump rings).

Fiber Art Bracelet

Metal and fiber are two very different elements that you'd rarely think to put together, but they work in this bracelet designed by Lori Larson. A plus to this project is that you don't need to have expert metalsmithing skills or loads of fiber knowledge to create this piece. It's easy and, other than waiting for glue to dry, relatively quick to make. Decide on your own selection of found metal objects, fibers, and beads to use, but follow the basic technique and you can quickly whip up some one-of-a-kind bracelets.

MATERIALS

- 1" × 6" (2.5 × 15.2 cm) brass or copper bracelet blank
- 1" (2.5 cm)-wide double-sided tape (such as Wonder Tape)
- metal brooch setting
- fibers
- 36" (91.4 cm) decorative wire
- choice of small beads and crystals
- found objects (such as washers and other hardware)
- E6000 glue
- skewer
- needle-nosed pliers

Designer's Tip

Walking is a great way to get a little inspiration and exercise at the same time. Consider taking a walk at a local park or beach, and keep a lookout for interesting objects you can combine into your mixed-media jewelry creations. A shell, an interesting twig, or a leaf can all be potential projects. If you prefer to walk around her neighborhood, tuck a few dollars into your pocket for the weekend yard sale you may stumble upon. You can almost guarantee you'll find old jewelry for sale that can be recycled into an objet d'art.

INSTRUCTIONS

1. Cover the entire bracelet blank with double-stick tape, and remove the backing to expose the adhesive.

2. Using E6000 glue, attach the metal brooch setting to the center of the bracelet and let dry.

3. Start wrapping fibers around the bracelet, working around the setting so as not to cover it up. While wrapping, make sure to press the ends of the fibers into the tape.

4. Use pliers to make a small loop on one end of the wire, string on your choice of beads onto the wire, and make another loop on the other end of the wire to help secure the beads.

5. Starting at one end of the bracelet and with the help of needle-nosed pliers, embed one end of the wire under the fibers and secure.

6. Continue by wrapping the wire around the entire bracelet, again working around the setting, and then embed the wire end on the other side of the bracelet.

7. To finish, glue on various found pieces of hardware, such as washers, to the top of the setting. Use the skewer to neatly apply the glue.

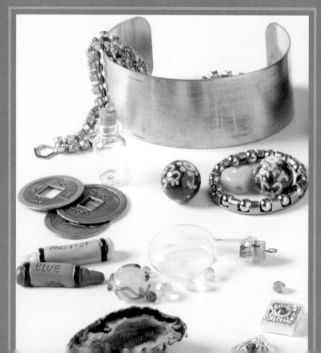

CHAPTER 4

Collectibles and Souvenirs

Pack rats feel vindicated when they begin dabbling in mixed media. Finally, they can use all the souvenirs and collections they have accumulated over the years to create jewelry pieces that are both beautiful and wearable. Beads and charms from old jewelry are wonderful elements to recycle into new jewelry pieces. Earrings that no longer have a partner, old toys, keys, coins, tokens, watch parts, and photos can be reborn into one-of-a-kind jewelry. Souvenir shopping while traveling is a great way to collect mementos. Rather than allow those trinkets to collect dust, use them in your jewelry. For those who don't leave home very often, souvenir items can also remind us of important events—the charm from a graduation tassel or a tiny bottle of hot sauce from an unforgettable meal. Turn your trip or event into a memory you can literally carry with you every day.

Timeless Treasure Pins

Once you finish making one of these pins, designed by Cyndi Lavin, you will understand how simple it is to create a treasured piece of jewelry out of discarded items. Adorned with odds and ends—broken jewelry, computer parts, wire pieces, leftover chain segments, discarded watch parts, and beads—each pin is a one-of-a-kind piece of miniature artwork. Leftover items collected over time make up the assembled elements arranged on lightweight Fome-Cor. Cover the entire pin in resin, attach a pin back, and wait impatiently for it to dry.

MATERIALS

- Fome-Cor
- metallic finishing wax (such as Rub 'n Buff)
- collected decorations (such as beads, broken jewelry, watches, wire, chains, charms, computer parts, etc.)
- pin back
- two-part epoxy resin
- utility blade
- pliers
- wire cutters
- tweezers
- two disposable mixing cups
- two small disposable paintbrushes
- waxed paper

INSTRUCTIONS

1. Determine the size and shape of pin, then use a utility blade to cut the Fome-Cor for the base of the pin.

2. Strip off the top and bottom layer of paper from the Fome-Cor, and stain it using a metallic finishing wax.

3. Arrange the beads and broken bits of jewelry, charms, computer parts, and other items collected on the Fome-Cor.

4. If any pieces have wires or sharp points, embed them into the Fome-Cor.

5. Mix up a small amount of epoxy resin into a disposable cup. Use a paintbrush to dab small drops of resin onto the backs of the collected items, and then position each onto the Fome-Cor.

6. Once all the pieces are attached to the Fome-Cor, carefully add a little more resin around them all.

7. Completely cover the top of the Fome-Cor, which now includes your selected collectibles, with a very thin layer of resin.

8. Let the pin dry on waxed paper overnight or until it is no longer tacky. Discard the cup and paintbrush after they are dry.

9. Mix another small amount of resin in a disposable cup, and paint a thin layer of resin onto the sides and back of the pin.

10. While the resin is tacky, position the pin back onto the back (the undecorated side) of the Fome-Cor. Let it dry on waxed paper overnight.

A Trip to Asia Necklace

Even if you can't jet off to some exotic location, that doesn't mean you can't dream about collecting special souvenirs on imaginary trips to far-off continents. This Asian-inspired necklace invokes a sense of timeless wanderings as rainbow-colored silky ribbon, red leather cord, gold-colored chain, and faux Oriental coins are mixed with Venetian glass gold-foil beads and Austrian aurora borealis (also referred to as AB) -enhanced red crystals. Keepsakes, especially anything with a hole such as old coins or unique beads, are easily adapted into jewelry with the aid of some wire, chain, ribbon, or leather.

MATERIALS

- five 22 mm faux Oriental coins with holes through the middle
- one rectangular 6 mm faux Oriental coin with hole at the top
- ten 6 mm Siam red AB Swarovski bicone crystal beads
- four 6 mm gold-foil Venetian glass beads
- one red gold-foil-lined Venetian glass tube-shaped bead
- 24" (61 cm) rainbow-colored ribbon
- 30" (76.2 cm) 3 mm red suede leather cord
- 22" (55.9 cm) gold-plated link chain
- ten 2" (5.1 cm) gold-colored head pins
- 36" (91.4 cm) 22-gauge (0.65 mm) gold-filled round wire
- round-nosed pliers
- flat-nosed pliers
- wire cutters
- jeweler's file
- corsage pin
- ruler
- scissors

Designer's Tip

One handy characteristic of a typical mixed-media artist is that of being a hoarder. You know—the type of person who hates to throw away anything—the type of person who thinks, "I could probably make something with this someday." And so, you tuck away that scrap of fabric, that piece of sea glass, or lone earring for inspiration to strike. If you aren't a hoarder, then it's time to become one as you begin to create your own collection of memorabilia. While you don't need to keep every little object that comes your way, if something speaks to you, then hold on to it. You never know when it will come in handy.

(continued from page 54)

INSTRUCTIONS

1. Measure about 7¹/₂" (19.1 cm) down from one end of the ribbon and tie an **overhand knot**.

2. Thread one 6 mm Venetian glass bead onto the other end of the ribbon, and push it down so it rests against the knot made in the step 1.

3. Use the **knot with bead** technique to tie another knot on the other side of the bead added in step 2.

4. Measure 2" (5.1 cm) from the last knot and repeat steps 1 through 3.

5. Measure 2" (5.1 cm) from the last knot and repeat steps 1 through 3, this time adding a red tube-shaped Venetian glass bead instead of the gold bead.

6. Repeat steps 1 through 4 to make the other side of the ribbon necklace strand, then set it aside while you work on the next strand.

7. Use the **mounting knot** technique to attach the leather cord to the rectangular Oriental faux coin. Also set this aside for later.

8. Using about 5" (12.7 cm) of gold-filled wire, insert the wire through the hole of one round coin and bend the wire so that approximately 1¹/₂" (3.8 cm) is on one side of the coin and the remaining wire is on the other side.

9. Hold the wire against the coin with your fingers, and with a pair of flat-nosed pliers in the other hand, use the **wire wrap** technique to wrap the shorter end of wire around the longer end of wire. The wire around the coin itself doesn't need to be tight.

10. Continue to wrap the wire until you have made three or four wraps, trim off excess wire, and use a jeweler's file to smooth the end.

11. Take the shorter piece of wire that is remaining, and use the **simple loop** technique to make a loop at the top of the coin.

12. Repeat steps 8 through 11 for the other four round coins.

13. Locate the center link of the chain, and attach one of the wire-wrapped coins onto this loop.

14. Count over nine links to either side of the middle link, and in the ninth link, add another coin. Repeat this until you have all five coins attached to the chain and there are eight links between each coin.

15. Thread one Siam crystal onto a head pin, and start a **wrapped loop**, but do not wrap the loop closed yet.

16. Count over two links past the last coin attached to the chain, slip the crystal dangle onto this link, and wrap the loop closed.

17. Continue creating crystal dangles and attaching them to the second link on the chain on each side of all five coins until you have a total of ten crystal dangles.

18. Insert more gold-filled wire through the last link on the chain, and connect it with a **wrapped loop**. Repeat this for the other side of the chain.

19. Pick up the ribbon and leather necklace strands previously made, and secure one end of the leather and ribbon together using an **overhand knot**. Repeat this for the other side of the strands. (Do not expect these strands to be the same length; instead, try to align their center areas—the leather with the coin and the ribbon with the tube bead. If necessary, adjust the position of the **overhand knot** and trim off excess ribbon or leather.)

20. Insert the wire on one end of the chain and through one of the **overhand knots** on the other strands.

21. Make a **wrapped loop** on the end of this wire, and use the widest end of the round-nosed pliers to make the loop extra-large. This will function as one side of your clasp.

22. Repeat step 20, this time making a **basic hook** on the end of the wire.

Sticks and Stones Set

Designer Theresa Mink's luxurious adjustable necklace, from 15" to 23" (38.1–58.4 cm), and long dangling earrings set is aptly titled *Sticks and Stones*, but don't let the name fool you. These aren't ordinary stones or everyday sticks. The stones are an assortment of gemstone beads: olive jade, carnelian, chalcedony, and mother-of-pearl. Her sticks are freshwater stick pearls. Along with these sticks and stones, she has incorporated crystals, glass, and vermeil pieces, all connected using gold-filled chains and findings.

Something Borrowed, Something Blue Bracelet

Borrow pieces of old earrings, collect left-over charms from discarded bracelets, and gather other gold-toned metal decorations for this busy mix of eclectic trinkets on a chain. The blue glass beads also have touches of gold to help these unrelated charms work together. Wire, chain, and a few findings are all you need to combine these pieces into a bracelet that jingles as it catches the light.

MATERIALS

- one 10 mm gold-plated toggle clasp
- eight various gold-colored charms
- six blue glass oval-shaped beads
- three blue glass coin-shaped beads
- six 2" (5.1 cm) gold-colored head pins
- 30" (76.2 cm) 22-gauge (0.65 mm) gold-filled round wire
- 7" (17.8 cm) gold-colored link chain
- round-nosed pliers
- flat-nosed pliers
- wire cutters
- jeweler's file

INSTRUCTIONS

1. Thread one coin bead on a head pin. Start a **wrapped loop** at the top of the head pin, and slide the loop of the head pin onto the second link before wrapping the loop closed.

2. Start a **wrapped loop** of wire, and slip a charm onto the loop before wrapping the loop closed.

3. Count down three links on the chain, and use the **wrapped loop** technique to connect the charm from step 2 to this third link.

4. Count over three more links, and repeat step 1, this time using an oval bead.

5. Continue the previous steps, alternating with a coin bead, charm, and oval bead until you have attached all the charms and all but two oval beads onto the chain.

6. Use more wire to start a **wrapped loop**, then attach it to one end of the chain before closing the loop.

7. Thread one oval bead onto the wire, make a **wrapped loop** on the other end of the wire, and slip on one side of the toggle clasp before closing the wrap.

8. Repeat step 7 to attach the other end of the toggle.

9. File any rough areas of the wire sections with a jeweler's file if necessary.

Grandmother's Marquee

Keep memories of your grandmother or other favorite relatives close to you by recycling their old jewelry pieces into fresh new jewelry. Because designer Victoria Button used recycled jewelry for this necklace, it may be difficult to find jewelry components that match exactly to the necklace pictured. Materials and techniques are included below as a guide for you to get started, but basically, this necklace is constructed by connecting old pieces of jewelry with wire, jump rings, and chain. Extra gemstones and crystal beads help make the jewelry components more cohesive in the final piece.

Designer's Tip

When making one-of-a-kind jewelry, especially mixed-media jewelry, it can be almost impossible to duplicate any given piece. That kind of jewelry is made in a factory and is considered "production work" in the art jewelry world. Therefore, take your own spin on the instructions to help you create your own original work. This concept is similar to cooking: You may see a chef on television create a dish, but you don't necessarily have all of the ingredients on hand. So, you improvise, using his or her method, but your own taste and available ingredients.

MATERIALS

- one 10 mm sterling toggle clasp
- two 2¹/₂" (6.4 cm) pieces medium-weight sterling chain
- four 24-gauge (0.51 mm) sterling 2" (5.1 cm) head pins
- two 6 mm sterling jump rings
- sixteen 4 mm sterling jump rings
- two matching pairs of large clip-on earrings
- one pair of smaller clip-on earrings
- one center jewelry component of your choice
- eight 4 mm aurora borealis clear crystal beads
- eighteen 4 mm sterling daisy spacer beads
- fourteen 4 mm faceted moss agate beads
- four 4 mm square fluorite beads
- 36" (91.4 cm) 21-gauge (0.72 mm) sterling wire
- two pairs of flat-nosed pliers
- round-nosed pliers
- heavy-duty wire cutters
- flush-cut wire cutters
- jeweler's file

Note: When disassembling costume jewelry, use a pair of heavy-duty wire cutters. The metal on some old jewelry may damage the blade on wire cutters normally intended for precious-metal wire such as sterling or gold-filled.

(continued from page 60)

INSTRUCTIONS

1. Begin by preparing the clip earrings and any other recycled pieces of jewelry. On the clip earrings, remove the paddle part of the clip, but leave the joint leg section (the piece of the clip that contains two holes). These holes will be used to attach wire and jump rings later on.

2. Now make the bead dangle and bead station sections for the necklace. Take a head pin, thread on one 4 mm faceted stone bead, one spacer bead, one crystal, another daisy, and another faceted stone bead. Make a **double loop** at the top of the head pin. Repeat this so that you have two dangle pieces, then set them aside for later use.

3. Make a **double loop** on one end of a piece of 21-gauge (0.72 mm) wire. Thread on one faced stone bead, one daisy bead, one crystal bead, one daisy bead, and another faceted stone bead. Finish the other end with another **double loop**. Repeat this so that you have two pieces, then set them aside for later use.

4. Repeat step 3, but use the following bead pattern: one square stone bead, one daisy, one faceted stone bead, one daisy, and another square stone bead. Set these aside for later use.

5. Make a **double loop** on one end of wire. Thread on one faceted stone bead, one daisy, one crystal, one daisy, and another faceted stone bead. Make a **wrapped loop** on the end of the wire.

6. Take a head pin, thread on one crystal and one daisy bead, and make a **wrapped loop** on the end of the head pin but, before wrapping the loop closed, attach it to the wrapped loop made in the previous step.

7. Repeat step 6 for a second dangle, and set this aside for later use.

8. Add wire to all of the recycled clip earrings and any other recycled jewelry pieces you want to include. Using 4" to 6" (10.2–15.2 cm) of 21-gauge (0.72 mm) wire, depending on the size of the earring, insert the wire through the holes in the joint leg section (which you left

on the jewelry pieces in step 1), and make **double loops** on both ends of the wire. This will secure the wire to the earring joint and also provide loops to use when assembling.

9. At this point, start assembling all of the jewelry components and prepared costume jewelry. Take a piece of chain and 6 mm jump ring. Using the **open jump ring** technique, slip on one end of the toggle clasp, and one end of the chain onto the ring. Then, use the **close jump ring** technique. Continue to use the **open** and **close jump ring** techniques throughout these instructions to attach each jewelry component to each other as you work your way down the necklace.

10. On the other end of the chain piece, use a 4 mm jump ring to attach a bead section from step 3.

11. With another 4 mm jump ring, attach a bead section made in step 4.

12. Attach the smallest earring component to the end of the previous bead section, using a 4 mm jump ring.

13. Repeat the step 12, this time using one of the large earring components.

14. Attach three 4 mm jump rings to the end of the earring component from the previous step. On the third jump ring, add another large earring.

15. Attach the center jewelry component of your choice to the previous earring, using a 4 mm jump ring.

16. To make the other side of the necklace, repeat steps 9 through 14. Attach this to the center jewelry component, using another jump ring.

17. Attach the dangles made in step 2 to the jump rings in between the two large earrings on one side of the necklace. Repeat this with the second dangle made in step 2 to the two large earrings on the other side of the necklace.

18. Attach the dangles made in steps 5 through 7 to the jump rings in between the large earring and the centerpiece on one side of the necklace. Repeat this on the other side of the necklace with the duplicate dangle.

Lovely Lucy Pendant

Lucille Ball gained her fame from being silly, but she was a very beautiful woman and talented actress, which is one reason why audiences were taken aback when she did wacky things like stomp around in a big vat of grapes or eat chocolates as they came down a conveyor belt. This necklace commemorates the physical beauty of this popular female comedian, though, of course, you could use this same design to salute your own favorite actress. Lori Larson combines a black-and-white image of Lucille Ball along with rubber stamping and metal fabrication techniques in this glam-gal necklace pendant design. After making the pendant, simply attach it to a sterling chain and feel like a glam-gal yourself when you wear it.

MATERIALS

- 1¹/₂" × 1¹/₂" (3.8 × 3.8 cm) 26-gauge (0.4 mm) copper plate
- small plastic container
- large plastic container with lid
- measuring cup
- ammonia
- salt
- sandpaper
- glossy clear spray sealant (such Krylon)
- adhesive (such as E6000)
- black embossing ink pad (such as Staz-On)
- text-style rubber stamp of your choice
- two 6 mm sterling jump rings
- 24" (61 cm) sterling link chain with attached clasp
- sterling "imagine" charm
- copper foil tape
- liver of sulfur
- cotton swab
- 1" × 1" (2.5 × 2.5 cm) clear glass square
- 1" × 1" (2.5 × 2.5 cm) acetate square
- metal hole punch
- two pairs of flat-nosed pliers

(continued from page 63)

INSTRUCTIONS

1. Punch a hole in the top and in the bottom of the metal plate, using the hole punch.

2. Sand one side of the copper plate, then set aside for later use.

3. Mix the patina solution by placing the smaller container, bottom side up, inside the larger container.

4. Pour approximately $1/2$ cup (118.3 ml) of ammonia into the bottom of the larger container.

5. Place the copper plate on top of the smaller container, sprinkle it with salt, and put the cover on the larger container, leaving it overnight.

6. The next day, remove the copper plate, rinse with water, and apply a spray sealant.

7. Once the sealant is dry, stamp the text stamp onto the copper piece, and set aside to dry.

8. Layer the glass square, image, and acetate so that the acetate is on the back. Place the copper foil tape around the pieces.

9. Use your finger to burnish the foil tape to ensure it is well sealed.

10. To blacken the copper tape, dip a cotton swab into liver of sulfur and apply it to the tape. (Follow the manufacturer's safety instructions when using chemicals such as liver of sulfur).

11. Glue the glass piece to the copper patina plate and allow to dry.

12. Use the **open** and **close jump ring** technique to attach the "imagine" charm to the bottom of the pendant and the sterling chain to the top of the pendant.

Memory Watch Case

An old watch case no longer has to be discarded. Instead, it can hold secret memories of a loved one. Designer Julia Andrus created this piece by combining tiny mementos of her grandmother and holding them together in an old watch case. The background of the case is a photograph (scanned and reprinted) of grandmother as a young woman, hair swept up and sporting a beautiful bonnet. The small watch parts included in the case move around with the beads reminding us that time does not stand still. All of this is connected with a jump ring to a vintage 32" (81.3 cm) jet bead necklace.

MATERIALS

- empty watch case
- miscellaneous watch parts
- your choice of small beads
- vintage photo image
- vintage jet necklace
- one 6 mm jump ring
- two pairs of pliers
- glue
- small hammer
- scissors
- towel

INSTRUCTIONS

1. Trim the vintage image with scissors to ensure it fits inside the watch case.

2. Glue the image inside the watch case and allow it to dry before continuing.

3. Fill the watch case with your choice of beads, watch parts, and any other small sentimental items that remind you of the person in the photo.

4. Close the watch case, wrap with a towel, and lightly tap the back of the case with a small hammer to secure.

5. Using the **open jump ring** and **close jump ring** techniques, attach the watch case (which now works as a pendant) with the jump ring in the center of the necklace.

Fabric Transfer Pillow Pendant

Image transfer is a wonderful method for combining photographs, photocopies, or clip art and re-engineering them, creating one-of-a-kind patterns on fabric. You can mix different images together to make a totally new one or use the originals as is. Either way, this interesting technique, incorporated in this pendant and necklace project by designer Julia Andrus, is a wonderful way to include unique images and color combinations into your mixed-media jewelry. Simple muslin fabric is transformed in this pillow pendant. Once you decide on your images and dye the muslin, use some silk cord and beads along with some basic jewelry-making techniques to construct this lightweight necklace. These instructions are designed as a model to follow, but you will make it your own when you select your choice of images and colors.

MATERIALS

- two 4" × 4" (10.2 × 10.2 cm) lightweight muslin squares
- lightweight batting
- 36" (91.4 cm) brown satin cord
- color photocopy of artwork
- two 2" (5.1 cm) gold-colored head pin
- one turquoise nugget bead
- three 8 mm brown glass pony beads
- five 6 mm copper glass pony beads
- one 8 mm amber glass oval bead
- one 10 mm copper toggle clasp
- two 2.75 mm gold-colored cord tips
- two 6 mm gold-colored jump rings
- permanent fabric adhesive (such as Fabric-Tac)
- dye sprays (such as Color Wash)
- powdered pigments (such as Perfect Pearls)
- image transfer medium (such as Perfect Fabric Medium)
- round-nosed pliers
- flat-nosed pliers
- paintbrush
- scissors
- scrap paper
- iron
- spray water bottle
- plastic bowl

Designer's Tip

To get a watercolor effect on dyed fabric, have a spray bottle of water handy. After dying the fabric, spray it with water and then blot with a paper towel. If you want to experiment or are working with spray dyes for the first time, practice on scrap muslin pieces. You may not use them later on in a piece of jewelry, but if you know you are just playing around and testing dye supplies, you don't have to worry if it doesn't turn out like you expect.

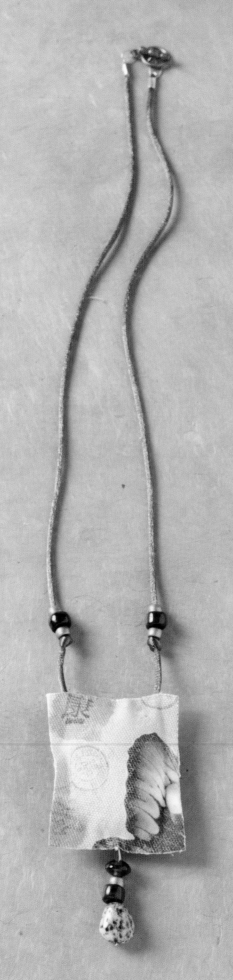

(continued from page 68)

INSTRUCTIONS

1. Cut out the selected artwork, leaving a 1/4" (6 mm) border around each one.

2. Using a paintbrush, apply fabric transfer medium to the front of the image, then quickly turn it facedown onto the middle of the muslin. Burnish it well, including the edges.

3. On the opposite side of the fabric (not the actual transfer), press with an iron on low heat to dry.

4. Place a scrap paper square about the same size as the transfer over the transfer, Cover the rest of the fabric cover with spray dye.

5. Use an iron or a heating tool to set the colors.

6. Remove the scrap paper, lightly spray the transfer with water, then begin rubbing in a circular motion to peel off the paper.

7. After removing as much paper as possible, dry it with an iron, and then spray it with more water to remove more paper. Repeat this until you remove all the paper.

8. In a plastic bowl, make a fabric glaze by mixing water, powdered pigments, and fabric medium.

9. With a paintbrush, apply the glaze over the entire piece. Blot the glaze with a paper towel if it is too heavy.

10. Repeat step 10 for the other muslin square, then set both using an iron.

11. Use scissors to trim the muslin squares to the size of the finished pendant.

12. Fold the satin cord in half and place it on the back muslin square in a V shape. The center of the cord should hang over the muslin just a little (this is what you'll attach the beaded dangle to later).

13. Apply fabric adhesive to the edges of the muslin, except for a small area at the top of both pieces. Spread the satin cord to the sides, and affix the front piece to the back. Pinch the edges to make a good seal, and allow it to completely dry before continuing.

14. In the top (unsealed) area of the muslin, use this as an entry point to stuff the pillow with batting.

15. Seal the top area with fabric adhesive.

16. Taking the head pin, add on one turquoise bead, one brown pony bead, one copper pony bead, and one glass amber bead, and make a **simple loop** at the top of the head pin.

17. Attach the head pin loop to the center of the satin cord on the bottom of the pillow. Use flat-nosed pliers to ensure the loop is closed around the cord.

18. Approximately 3/4" (1.9 cm) from the top of the pillow, tie an **overhand knot** on the satin cord. Repeat this for the other side of the satin cord.

19. On one side of the cord, string on one copper pony bead, one brown pony bead, and another copper pony bead.

20. Make sure the satin cord is about the length you want, trim off any excess, insert the end of the cord inside a cord tip, and use flat-nosed pliers to flatten the cord tip.

21. Repeat steps 19 and 20 for the other side of the satin cord.

22. Attach a jump ring and then one side of the toggle clasp to both cord tips.

Fabric Transfer Pillow Pendant

A color photocopier is perfect for making copies of artwork to later transfer onto fabric, and that's just what mixed-media artist Julia Andrus did for this fabric pillow pendant. After transferring the image onto muslin, she used water and paper towels to smear the image just a little in order to fade it and trimmed the edges of the material. The water gives the final pendant a watercolor effect. To attach the leather cord, she affixed it to the muslin before adding a second piece of fabric to cover it. Then, just as one might with a standard sewn pillow, Julia stuffed it and embellished the strap with a mixture of metal and glass beads. The final dangle in the middle is attached to the center of the leather cord that she allowed to peek out through the bottom of the pillow.

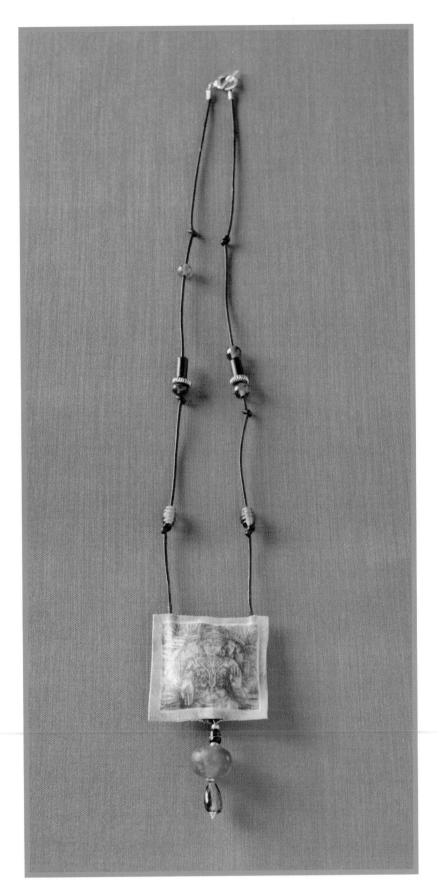

CHAPTER 5

Found Objects and Natural Materials

If you are already a natural collector of pretty things, then you have an edge when it comes to learning to make mixed-media jewelry. Everyday items you tend to pick up and save—bottle caps, antique hardware, colorful aluminum or tin cans—become design elements in your new jewelry creations. Nature is also a wonderful resource for shells, bones, coral, colorful pebbles, and even twigs that cost you nothing. Combine found objects and natural materials with traditional jewelry components such as wire, findings, and beads, and you will be amazed at what you can come up with. If you aren't already a collector, no worries—this is a perfect excuse to go for a solo walk on the beach or take the kids out for a walk through your local park. Keep your eyes open for colors and textures that appeal to you, and soon you'll have a varied collection of found and natural objects to inspire your future jewelry pieces.

Day at the Beach Necklace

Crystals, sterling, and shells mixed together result in earthy elegance for this necklace designed by Lisa Lampe. The finished necklace is approximately 18" (45.7 cm) but you can alter the length by simply adding or subtracting chain segments that are used to connect the unusual assortment of jewelry components. Lisa selected a square lampwork bead enhanced with Boro Bora frit, a mixture of tiny glass fragments which, when heated, react with a burst of golden undertones. The focal bead is where you can add your own personal statement by selecting a bead that has special meaning to you.

MATERIALS

- one 12 mm square Boro Bora lampwork bead
- two 12 mm sterling daisy spacer beads
- two 12 mm faceted smoky quartz rondelle beads
- nine sliced spiral shell beads
- twenty 4 mm heishi shell beads
- twelve 4 mm Swarovski bicone Erinite AB crystals
- one 6 mm Swarovski bicone Erinite AB crystal
- one 12 mm sterling toggle clasp
- two 6 mm sterling split rings
- two 1¹/₂" (3.8 cm) head pin
- four 4 mm sterling corrugated rondelle beads
- two 2 × 2 mm sterling crimp beads
- 8" (20.3 cm) 0.024 mm beading wire
- 24" (61 cm) 22-gauge (0.65 mm) sterling wire
- approximately 6" (15.2 cm) large-link (6 mm) sterling chain
- two 15 mm diamond-shaped sterling links
- four 8 mm diamond-shaped sterling links
- round-nosed pliers
- wire cutters
- flat-nosed pliers
- crimping pliers

(continued from page 74)

INSTRUCTIONS

1. Cut off a section of large-link chain so that you have nine links, each approximately 2" (5.1 cm) long.

2. Using sterling wire, make a **wrapped loop**, but before closing the loop, slide it onto one end of the chain cut in the previous step.

3. Thread a 4 mm crystal onto the wire, and again begin a **wrapped loop**, but before closing it, attach one 8 mm diamond-shaped sterling link onto the loop.

4. Take more wire and make another **wrapped loop**, attaching it to the other end of the diamond-shaped link in the previous step before closing the loop.

5. Thread one 4 mm crystal, one 4 mm corrugated rondelle bead, ten heishi beads, another rondelle, and another crystal onto the wire, and make a **wrapped loop** on the end, but before closing the wrap, attach an 8 mm diamond-shaped link to the loop.

6. Take another four links of the large chain, select the second link on the chain piece, and attach the **wrapped loop** to this piece. This leaves an extra link of chain that will be used later.

7. Make another **wrapped loop**, and attach it to the end of the chain piece formed in the previous step.

8. Thread on a 4 mm crystal, make a **wrapped loop**, and attach a 15 mm diamond-shaped link to the end of the loop before wrapping it closed.

9. Repeat steps 1 through 5 to start the other side of the necklace.

10. Repeat step 6, but instead of selecting the second link on the chain, connect the **wrapped loop** piece to the first link.

11. Repeat steps 7 and 8.

12. For the extra link dangling from step 6, take a head pin, thread on one 6 mm crystal, make a **wrapped loop**, and attach this to the dangling link before wrapping the loop closed.

13. Repeat step 12, but this time, thread on a sliced spiral shell bead onto the head pin before attaching it to the dangling link.

14. To create the centerpiece that will attach both necklace pieces previously made, insert some beading wire through and around the end of the 15 mm diamond-shaped links. Attach a **crimp bead** onto the beading wire.

15. Thread on one 4 mm crystal bead, four spiral shell beads, one smoky quartz bead, one 12 mm daisy spacer bead, the square lampwork bead, another daisy spacer, another smoky quartz, four more spiral shell beads, one 4 mm crystal bead, and the last crimp bead.

16. Insert the beading wire through and around the end of the other 15 mm diamond-shaped link on the other section of necklace, and secure the **crimp bead**.

17. To attach the toggle, slip a spring ring on one end of the chain section of the necklace, and slip one side of the toggle onto the same spring ring. Repeat this for the other side of the necklace.

Shell Melange

Shells in all shapes and sizes are mixed with a touch of crystal sparkle and earthy gemstone elements in this similar necklace created by glass artist and jewelry designer, Lisa Lampe. Another layer of texture comes from the different sterling components arranged throughout the piece, from corrugated rondelle beads to large chain link sections. A whimsical addition to the necklace includes a glittery starship, which Lisa made herself using lampworking techniques.

Pop Culture Earrings

We are a pop culture, and the evidence to testify to this fact is located in our recycling bins. One clever crafter, Shannon Jefferson, decided to turn trash into trinkets in the form of these colorful soda pop earrings. Discarded aluminum cans become popular fashion statements with a few supplies and some alternative jewelry-making techniques. For these earrings, eyelets are used to attach ear hooks and dangles.

MATERIALS

- one aluminum soda can
- one pair of sterling ear hooks
- two plastic cherry charms
- two 6 mm sterling jump rings
- six $1/16$" (1.6 mm) eyelets in different colors
- two $1/8$" (3 mm) eyelets
- $1/16$" (1.6 mm) hole punch
- $1/8$" (3 mm) hole punch
- eyelet setter
- tin snips
- fine-grit sandpaper
- protective gloves
- small metal hammer
- two pairs of flat-nosed pliers

Note: Be extra careful when working with the sharp aluminum. Wear protective gloves.

INSTRUCTIONS

1. Puncture the side of the aluminum can with tin snips, creating a hole that is large enough to cut all the way around the can.

2. Cut out a large piece of aluminum from the can. While cutting, do not close the snips all the way down, to avoid fraying the metal.

3. Use your hands (you should be wearing gloves) to flatten the aluminum, and then cut out two rectangular pieces that are approximately $1^1/4$" (3.2 cm) long and $1/2$" (1.3 cm) wide.

4. File all edges of the rectangles with fine-grit sandpaper.

5. Using the **metal eyelet** technique, attach one $1/16$" (1.6 mm) eyelet to the top and one $1/8$" (3 mm) eyelet to the bottom of each rectangle.

6. Add two more decorative eyelets to the center of each rectangle.

7. Use the **open** and **close jump ring** techniques to attach the cherry charms to the bottom of each rectangle.

8. With pliers, open the loop of an ear hook, slip the hook onto the top eyelet, and close the loop. Repeat this to finish the second earring.

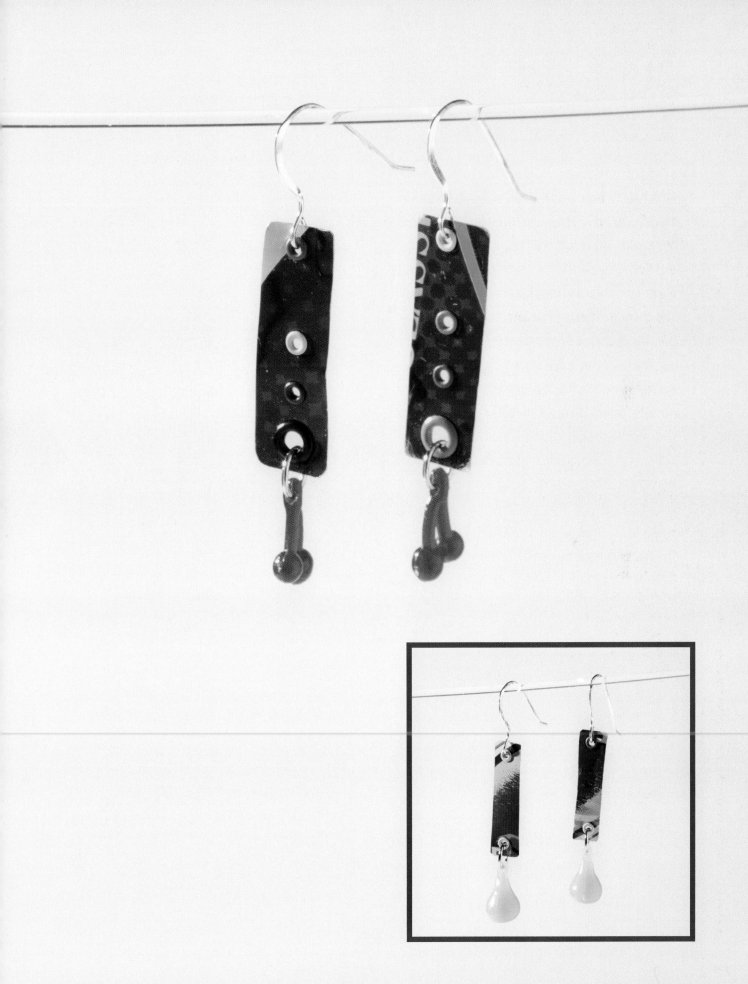

Coral Tie Bracelet

Bead stringing often does not get the artistic kudos it deserves. While the basic techniques of bead stringing are simple—bead, thread, and finish with clasp—it takes more than the basics to make a beaded jewelry piece interesting. Phaedra A. Torres takes an imaginative approach to her bead stringing, which includes the fairly simple techniques of crimping and knotting. This coral bracelet is a wonderful example of her design methods, taking items such as buttons, resin beads, and glass beads, and attaching them to the coral and crystal beaded bracelet, using scraps of suede intermittently throughout the jewelry piece. The quirky combination of these simple techniques takes bead stringing to another level.

MATERIALS

- 10" (25.4 cm) of 12 mm coral disc beads
- eight 6 mm olivine Czech glass beads
- two 2" (5.1 cm) sterling head pins
- one 10 mm sterling toggle clasp
- two 2 × 2 mm crimp beads
- 12" (30.5 cm) 0.019 mm beading wire
- your choice of glass, wood, resin beads
- your choice of buttons
- 12" (30.5 cm) olive-colored suede lace
- scissors
- crimp beads
- wire cutters
- round-nosed pliers

Designer's Tip

One of the first elements to consider when collecting found objects or souvenirs for a jewelry piece is whether or not it comes with a hole. Buttons are perfect, of course, because they either have a few holes in the middle or a shank on the back. You can string them directly onto a piece with beading wire, or you can use fibers or wire to attach them. With fibers, **overhand** or **square knots** work well. Wire is useful because you can create a bale using the **wrapped loop** method. If there is no hole, consider wrapping wire around the entire piece or gluing on metal bales or jump rings. There are lots of different ways to attach unusual items to jewelry, but look first for a hole before deciding how you will incorporate a piece into the finished jewelry design.

(continued from page 80)

INSTRUCTIONS

1. Insert the end of the beading wire through the loop on one side of the toggle clasp, and attach a **crimp bead**.

2. String on two Czech crystals, and approximately 1¹/₄" (3.2 cm) of coral beads.

3. Take some suede, string on your choice of beads and buttons, and use an **overhand knot** to secure the bead and button to the suede, making sure to leave extra tails of suede.

4. Attach the suede tails to the beading wire after the coral beads, using a **square knot**. Trim off excess suede.

5. String on about ¹/₂" (1.3 cm) more of coral beads. Repeat steps 3 and 4.

6. Repeat step 5 three more times, and then string on another 1¹/₄" (3.2 cm) of coral beads and two more Czech crystals.

7. Repeat step 1 to attach the other side of the toggle clasp, and use wire cutters to trim off excess beading wire.

8. Take one head pin, thread on three Czech crystals, and make a **simple loop** at the top of the head pin.

9. Connect this crystal head pin to the loop on the circular part of the toggle clasp.

10. Take the other head pin, thread on one Czech crystal and approximately ¹/₂" (1.3 cm) of coral beads.

11. Make a **simple loop** at the top of the head pin, and connect this to the circular part of the toggle clasp to complete the bracelet.

Jean Harlow Hardware Necklace

Known as the "Original Blond Bombshell," Jean Harlow was the goddess of Hollywood, the first actress to show that the stereotype of the innocent blonde can be deceiving. She is immortalized in this whimsical necklace designed and constructed by Lori Larson, who combined funky found objects such as a bottle cap, a ball-bearing caster, and some rubber tubing with glam and glitter. Hardware store finds are fun to transform into unexpected jewelry designs. Combined with paper, glue, and your imagination, you can create your own little bit of Hollywood-meets-hardware style of jewelry.

MATERIALS

- 1" × 1" (2.5 × 2.5 cm) precut piece of glass
- glossy paper
- small clip art of Jean Harlow
- decorative paper with text on it
- silver foil tape
- bottle cap
- Diamond Glaze
- E6000 glue
- metal hole punch
- one 6 mm jump ring
- 20" (50.8 cm) ball chain with fastener
- one flat-back "love" charm
- one flat-back clear crystal
- two 1" (2.5 cm) pieces of clear rubber tubing
- one ball-bearing caster
- scissors
- glue stick
- foam brush
- two pairs of pliers

Designer's Tip

Old movie-star images are great ways to include photographs in your mixed-media art, but don't forget your own family as well. New photographs can look vintage by scanning them using a flatbed scanner and then printing them in black and white. You can also try playing around with software, such as Adobe Photoshop, to change the tints or to color-enhance images. If you don't feel technically savvy, there's always the option of photocopying the images on a black-and-white photocopier. You can also use colored pencils to color in areas for an artful effect.

(continued from page 83)

INSTRUCTIONS

1. Cut the clip art to fit inside the bottle cap. Cover the back with glue from the glue stick, and press into the center of the bottle cap.

2. Use Diamond Glaze and a small foam brush to cover the clip art, and let dry.

3. With a metal hole punch, make a hole at the top of the bottle cap.

4. Use E6000 glue to adhere the bottle cap to the inside of the caster, and set aside for later use.

5. Cut a piece of decorative paper and glossy paper to fit over the precut piece of glass.

6. Sandwich the glass, then decorative paper, then glossy paper together so that the glossy paper is the last piece and the decorative paper is visible through the glass.

7. Hold the paper and glass pieces together and cover the edges with silver foil tape, sticky side against the pieces. Trim off excess foil.

8. Again with E6000 glue, attach the bottle cap piece created in steps 1 through 4 to the corner of the glass and paper piece, and allow to dry.

9. Continue to glue on a flat-back crystal onto a flat-back "love" charm, and then glue this entire piece to the other corner of the glass and paper piece.

10. While the pendant is drying, cut two small pieces of decorative paper, roll up the paper tightly, and insert them into the two pieces of tubing.

11. Use the **open** and **close jump ring** technique to attach a jump ring to the hole in the pendant. Thread the chain through a rubber tube bead, through the jump ring, then through another rubber tube bead to complete the necklace.

Fire Screen Earrings

The miracle of paint is that it can make just about anything look better. In this project, designed by D. Lynn Reed, paint, wire, and beads transform simple fire screen into lovely dangling earrings. The holes in the screen are perfect for connecting beads and ear hooks. If desired, shape the screen before painting with the aid of a wood dapping block and rounded wood dye, to give the screen pieces a slightly curved shape.

MATERIALS

- metal fire screen grate scraps
- heat-set paints in fuchsia and white (such as Pébéo or Liquitex)
- two 24-gauge (0.51 mm) 2" (5.1 cm) sterling head pins
- two 4 mm fuchsia bicone beads
- two 4 mm white pearls beads
- two 2 mm sterling beads
- pair of large sterling kidney ear wires
- round-nosed pliers
- wire cutters
- scissors
- jeweler's file
- small paintbrush
- toaster oven

INSTRUCTIONS

1. Use scissors to cut out two $1/2$" × $1/2$" (1.3 × 1.3 cm) squares from the screen, making sure that a hole is available at the center top and center bottom of each square.

2. Use a jeweler's file all around the squares to remove any rough areas.

3. Apply paints to the front of each screen piece. Following the manufacturer's instructions, cure the pieces into a toaster oven dedicated to creating art (so as not to taint your food).

4. Once the paint is dry, take a head pin and string on one crystal, one pearl, and one silver bead.

5. Make a **wrapped loop** at the top of the head pin, and before wrapping it closed, slip it through the bottom center hole in one piece of screen.

6. Take a kidney ear wire, open the hooked part of the wire, and slide the screen piece using the top center hole to secure to the ear wire.

7. Repeat steps 4 through 6 for the second earring.

Patina Doodad Pin

Designer Lori Larson lives near an industrial park where she often finds objects such as old screws and metal items of unidentifiable origins. Instead of considering them just junk, these found objects inspire her to create all kinds of unique mixed-media jewelry pieces such as this pin. To give the copper a well-worn look that mixes well with the odds and ends she finds, Lori has developed a simple recipe for transforming a shiny piece of copper into a patina piece of metal. Use her method to make your own pin, and then move on to developing other jewelry objects that have an industrialized look to them.

MATERIALS

- 2 1/2" × 1 1/2" (6.4 × 3.8 cm) 26-gauge (0.4 mm) copper plate
- pin back
- assortment of metal decorations (such as washers, wire, etc.)
- small plastic container
- large plastic container with lid
- measuring cup
- ammonia
- salt
- sandpaper
- glossy clear spray sealant (such as Krylon)
- adhesive (such as E6000)

INSTRUCTIONS

1. Sand one side of the copper plate, and set aside for later use.
2. Mix the patina solution by placing the smaller container, bottom side up, inside the larger container.
3. Pour approximately 1/2 cup (118.3 ml) of ammonia into the bottom of the larger container.
4. Place the copper plate on top of the smaller container, and sprinkle it with salt.
5. Place the cover on the larger container and leave overnight.
6. The next day, remove the copper plate, rinse with water, and apply a spray sealant.
7. Once the sealant is dry, glue on your choice of flat-back decorative items to the copper plate. Add glue to the back of the decorations and adhere to the front of the copper plate.
8. Let the adhesive dry, and then glue the pin back to the back of the copper plate piece.

Bone Collector Necklace

Ancient bone collectors are known for collecting dragon bones for their powers, and designer Yolanda Odom isn't really that different from these ancient wizards. Bits of leftover yarn and odds and ends came directly from her studio stash. She found the centerpiece one day while walking in the woods. Obviously, since Yolanda's necklace is a conglomeration of pieces collected over many years, this project is more of a technique to follow rather than a blueprint to copy. The method used in this necklace is stringing, and lots of dangle elements add to its magic. You can concoct your own magic by using your own collection of jewelry components: wood, bone, glass, wire, and fibers.

Designer's Tip

Make your own paper beads by recycling old newspapers or pages from a discarded book. (Check your local library for books they are throwing out or selling for cheap.) Cut the paper into long triangular strips, and, starting at the wider end, roll the paper around a knitting needle. Continue to roll until about an inch from the end and then dab some glue on the paper to close it. Coat the bead with a few layers of acrylic gel medium to seal.

MATERIALS

- one vertebrae bone for pendant
- four 20 mm paper tube beads
- 10 grams of size 11 black seed beads
- 10 grams of size 8 gray seed beads
- 12" (30.5 cm) black leather cord
- 26" (66 cm) 19-gauge (0.91 mm) stainless-steel wire
- 24" (61 cm) black and gold eyelash yarn
- one 10 mm bone bead
- eighteen 6 mm carved wooden beads
- thirty 8 mm painted wooden beads
- four 15 mm barrel bone beads
- two 25 mm carved bone tube beads
- two 10 mm carved hexagon bone beads
- fourteen 10 mm bone disc beads
- two 15 mm brown wooden disc beads
- ten 4 mm black glass disc beads
- ten 4 mm red glass disc beads
- one 4 mm yellow glass disc bead
- 24" (61 cm) 0.019 mm beading wire
- heavy-duty wire cutters
- round-nosed pliers
- flat-nosed pliers
- bench block
- chasing hammer
- black Silamide beading thread
- size 10 beading needle
- scissors
- G-S Hypo Cement
- tape

(continued from page 90)

INSTRUCTIONS

1. Make the bead and wire dangles to add later during stringing by using round-nosed pliers to curl the end of a few inches of wire into a coil.

2. Set the wire on a bench block. Use a chasing hammer to lightly hammer to flatten the coil of wire.

3. Thread one red glass bead, one painted wood bead, and another red glass bead onto the wire. Use round-nosed pliers to curl the other end of the wire. Trim off excess wire as necessary.

4. Repeat steps 1 through 3 for another matching dangle, and set both aside for later use.

5. Repeat the above steps, this time using a little more wire, string on one red glass bead, one paper bead, and another red glass bead before curling the end. Do this again to have two matching beaded dangles.

6. Repeat the above techniques one more time, this time using even more wire and thread on one red bead, one paper bead, one yellow bead, one paper bead, and one red bead before curling the end. Set all dangles aside for later use.

7. Now insert wire through the hole in one brown wooden disc bead, and make a **wrapped loop** to secure the bead to the wire.

8. With excess wire, make a **simple loop** at the top of the bead, repeat this to make a duplicate wood disc dangle, and set both aside for later use.

9. Put together the bone and bead pendant by securing the leather through the center top of the bone with a **mounting knot**.

10. Wrap one strand of the leather again through the hole in the bone, secure to the bottom part of the bone using an **overhand knot**, and repeat this for the other strand of leather for the other side of the bone piece.

11. Cross leather strands, and use an **overhand knot** to attach both pieces of leather to the opposite sides of the bone piece.

12. On one strand of leather, string on three painted wooden beads, tie the end of the leather with an **overhand knot**, cut off excess leather, and repeat this for the other leather strand.

13. For the black seed bead embellishments on the bone, thread the beading needle with Silamide, add a piece of tape to the end of the thread (to keep beads from falling off), and string on about forty seed beads. (The number of seed beads will vary, depending on the size of the bone).

14. Insert the strand of beads through the top hole of the bone. With both pieces of thread on either side of the seed beads, tie a **square knot**.

15. Dab some Hypo Cement onto the knot and trim off excess thread.

16. Repeat steps 13 through 15 for another beaded embellishment positioned so that it mirrors the first on the bone piece.

17. Take the three paper dangles previously made, and connect them to the leather area that is across the front of the bone piece.

18. Take beading wire, and thread it through the leather and seed bead embellishments at the top of the bone pendant. Pull the beading wire until the pendant is in the center of the wire.

19. Add more tape to one end of the beading wire, and start stringing on beads and dangles on the other side, alternating wood, bone and glass beads, and adding the leftover dangles until you have about 10" (25.4 cm) of beads strung. Duplicate the pattern you've created on the other side of the necklace. On the necklace shown, the larger bone beads are closer to the center of the necklace.

20. To make one side of the toggle, thread on one 10 mm bone bead, one 4 mm red glass bead, and four gray seed beads.

21. Thread the end of the beading wire back through these last beads added, skipping the gray seed bead, tie an **overhand knot** with the beading wire, dab some glue on the knot, and push the beads on the strand over the knot before the glue is dry.

22. To make the loop part of the toggle, on the other side of the necklace, thread on twenty-four gray seed beads, and insert the beading wire through the first seed bead.

23. Pull the beaded loop, and before finishing, make sure the loop fits around the 10 mm bone bead added in step 20. Adjust the beaded loop as necessary by adding or removing seed beads to make sure it fits snuggly around the bone bead.

24. Tie an **overhand knot** after the last seed bead, glue, let dry, and then **wire wrap** a length of steel wire around the knot to secure and cover it.

Variation Idea

Cocoon Necklace

A vintage silver spoon is the center-piece of this found-object necklace. Mixed-media artist Stephanie Lee used a saw to cut out the center and handle of the spoon and then drilled holes into it. Like a seam-stress sewing with wire, she laced thin copper wire back and forth through the holes and attached a piece of embellished mica. The chain is also vintage, and she used more copper wire to attach this to the top of the spoon along with dangles of crystal, coral, and glass beads. Two etched nickel tags are also included, both in the center of the spoon and as a dangle from the end of the chain.

CHAPTER 6

Mixed-Media Jewelry Gallery

Now for the Mixed-Media Jewelry Gallery—packed full of awesome jewelry designs from a wide range of talented artist who have their own distinct mixed-media flair. Through experimentation and trial and error they have developed many of their signature techniques. Sit back, enjoy, and become inspired!

Mellow Yellow
by Theresa Mink Designs

The colors of autumn were the inspiration for the necklace designed by jewelry maker Theresa Mink. Gold-filled chain and a wire-wrapped hook allow for easy adjustability, from 18" to 24" (45.7–61 cm). The centerpiece is a highly polished 46 mm mother-of-pearl pendant. Doubled strands of gold-filled chain are connected together using a mixture of light and earthy beads, including yellow jade, mother-of-pearl, olive jade, glass, and bone. The chain and mother-of-pearl pendant, which is also accented with glass and pearl dangle elements, are connected with a textured gold-filled center ring.

Peaches and Cream Set
by Theresa Mink Designs

The peach color of coral is a perfect addition to white Biwa stick pearls and gold-filled beads and findings in the necklace and earring set by jewelry designer Theresa Mink. The necklace is approximately 18" (45.7 cm) long and, along with freshwater stick pearls and slivers of graduated coral pieces, it includes 4 mm freshwater pearls, small chunky coral beads, and 4 mm gold-filled spacer beads. The hook includes a gold-filled wrapped hook and jump ring. Matching earrings dangle from gold-filled posts and contain freshwater stick and round pearls, golf-filled components and beads, and coral side-drilled teardrop beads.

In Stereo Bracelet
by Sherri Forrester

Old stereos are more than just a freebie to give to the local thrift store, and jewelry designer Sherri Forrester proves their worth in this stereo-style bracelet. She began by making a base for her stereo-scrap finds. First, using seed beads and basic bead-weaving techniques, she made a simple woven bracelet with extra loops to allow it to adjust from 6" to 7" (15.2–17.8 cm). Even part of the toggle is from an old stereo. Then it was time to adorn the basic bracelet form with stereo dangles, which she scattered randomly across the bracelet and attached using wire that was already connected to the stereo pieces.

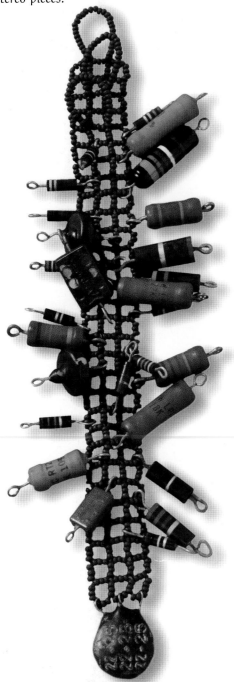

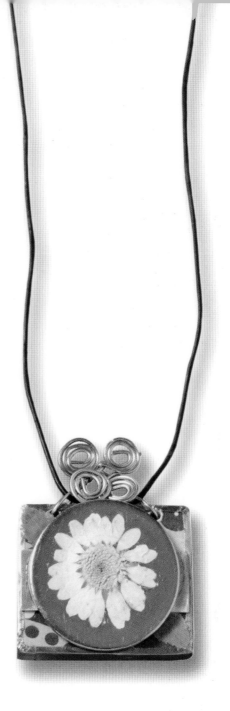

Copper Daisy
by Vickie Zumpf

Crafting methods mix it up in this daisy pendant by Vickie Zumpf. The base of the pendant is wood. On top of that is layered an assortment of decorative papers, a metal washer, and a dried daisy flower. The copper foil framing this piece is the same used for stained glass. Finally the top of the pendant is adorned with coils of copper, which combine function (it works as a bale for the attached leather cord) and fashion (the coils together resemble the shape of a flower).

Wrapped in Love
by Gretchen S. Sarrazolla

In the center of the sterling wire heart pendant is a beach rock the artist found. The heart and bale are formed from sterling silver round wire, and then the heart is textured by using a metal hammer to purposefully mark the metal. The multistrand strap includes suede, leather, black beading wire enhanced with stations of sterling beads, and organza ribbon. The five strands are captured at the ends with sterling tornado-style crimps that finish off the ends of the fibers as well as provide a place to attach a sterling lobster-claw clasp. Finally, a chain with a dangle of jasper on the end allows the wearer to adjust the size of the necklace.

By the Sea
by Jaimee Jo Hatt

Designer Jaimee Hatt collected the shells for this neck-lace on a stretch of beach that was once a favorite childhood destination. The white shells have a pearly oysterlike sheen, which inspired her to complement them with 4 mm white freshwater pearl beads. She connected each shell to the pearl strand, using clear monofilament and crimp beads. The clasp consists of a sterling jump ring and basic hook made from round sterling silver wire. The length is approximately 18" (45.7 cm).

Luxe Jewels Mixed-Media Necklace
by Maya Brenner

Jewelry designer Maya Brenner used a basic stringing technique for this 29" (73.7 cm) necklace, but the materials incorporated into this piece are anything but basic. Three large (16 mm) hemp beads are the most unique materials for this long necklace and are spaced asymmetrically throughout the strand. The other eclectic mixture of beads include 10 mm lacy filigree metal beads, 6 × 18 mm oval-shaped wooden beads, 6 mm yellow jade beads, 8 mm red aventurine coin-shaped beads, and size 11 glass seed beads. The ends are finished with a crimp bead and include a sterling jump ring and lobster-claw clasp.

Bottle Link Necklace
by Carol Kemp for Carol K. Originals

The tiny glass bottle, which is the focal piece for this chain, wire, and bead necklace, contains an assortment of secrets: shredded paper, miscellaneous beads, and metal pieces. Designer Carol Kemp is the only person privy to the true meaning of her necklace design. The strap is a combination of hand-formed wire loops, which are wrapped together, chain, and bead sections. Two tones of blue beads include turquoise and lapis lazuli. The extra tiny dangles hanging from the bottle in the center include peridot chips and blue crystals. The necklace length is approximately 20" (50.8 cm) and is finished off with a sterling lobster-claw clasp.

Dance the Night Away
by Opie O'Brien

Artist Opie O'Brien was inspired by craft store purchases as well as hardware store finds when designing this pendant. Materials include silver-colored craft store sheet metal, a vintage tin lithographic, various finishes and sizes of metal eyelets, clear Plexiglas, and a blue cabochon. The image used from this piece came from a vintage tin can, and to add to the festive Spanish theme, Opie shaped the top of the metal frame into a scalloped fan. On the back, a metal bale is hidden from view, but it is also made from a decorative vintage tin. The entire pendant is secured together in layers with eyelets, much like those you'd find in the scrapbook aisle of your local craft store.

Sparkling Patina Pendants

by Lori Larson

Nothing goes to waste in Lori Larson's mixed-media studio. Scraps of copper sheet metal are perfect for creating a patina finish on and then using as the canvas for her found-object collage jewelry pieces. In the pendants pictured, Lori incorporated nails and washers and then topped them off with large sparkling sequins. One piece includes text from a label machine, and a simple sterling jump ring bale. The other pendant includes a more ornate bale made from a jump ring attached to the copper pendant, and then an eye-pin is inserted through a silver Bali-style cone component. Both are hung on black rubber cord.

Booklace Necklace

by Carol Kemp

Paper, foil, leather, and beads are transformed into wearable book art when artist Carol Kemp starts creating with them. This small book pendant is made from watercolor paper and purple-colored foil. Inside its cover is a tiny accordion booklet with itty-bitty envelope pockets so you can tuck in a tiny note to yourself or stash a favorite fortune cookie message. Copper wire is attached to the spine of the booklet, and then these wire loops are attached to leather cord, which is embellished with blue glass beads and metal tube spacer beads. The button-style bead on top of the book is also glass.

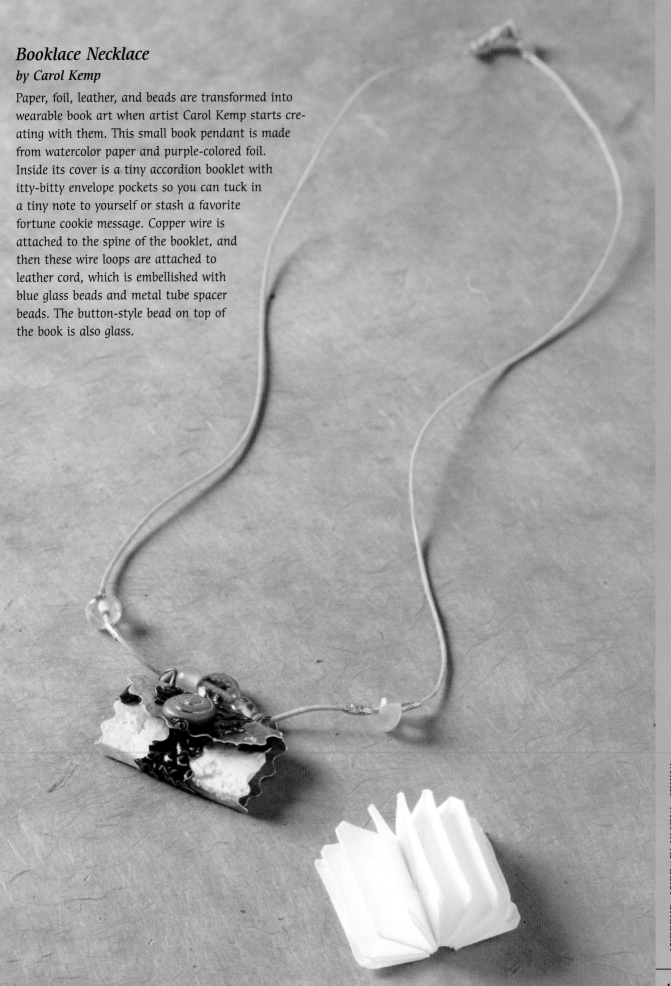

Double Button Whimsy Pins
by Elizabeth Dickinson

Not one but two buttons are used for each
of these whimsical pin designs constructed by mixed-media artist
Elizabeth Dickinson. Glass,
metal, and plastic buttons are
stacked together, starting with
the longer plastic colored button
on the bottom. A length of sterling
round wire is threaded through the
wholes in the buttons and then twisted
to connect them. Dickinson then twists and
curls and shapes the wire into spirals and free-
form shapes, adding other embellishments
such as crystal and glass beads. Finally, a pin
finding is glued to the back or jump rings are
attached to the wire sections to make them
into pendants.

Vintage Embellishments
by Michela Verani

Old sterling pins become new, modernized
pieces after jewelry artist Michela Verani is
finished with them. Rather than taking the
vintage pins apart, Michela keeps them as is
and uses sterling wire and coated beading
wire to attach an assortment of colorful
beaded dangles. These dangles continue the
nature theme that is already part of the original sterling pin design. Her choice of beads
includes green and white freshwater stick
pearls; glass flower and glass leaf beads in
various designs; and glass seed beads.

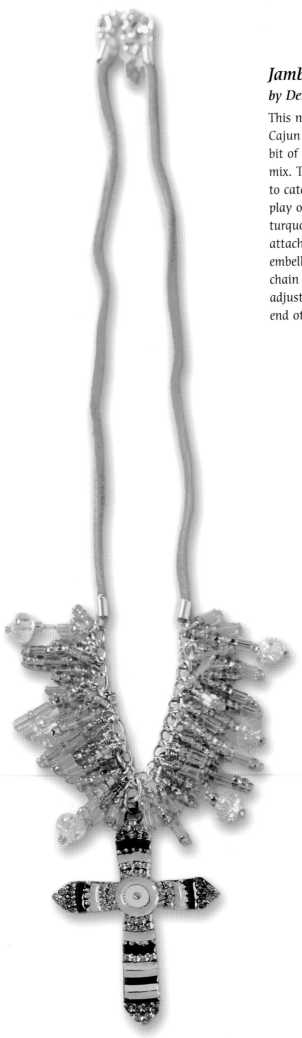

Jamble Necklace
by Denise Witmer

This necklace design is reminiscent of the famous Cajun dish jambalaya because it consists of a little bit of everything tossed together to create a delicious mix. The enamel cross pendant is the first ingredient to catch your eye. Then loads of glass beaded dangles play off the colors of the pendant. The strap is turquoise-colored leather lace with sterling coils attached to both ends to connect it to the center of embellished chain. Designer Denise Witmer used chain again on one end of the necklace to make it adjustable. The final touch is another dangle on the end of this chain section.

Three-Washer Necklace and Mother-of-Pearl Washer Necklace
by Elizabeth Dickinson

Washers get a makeover with sparkles, wire, and beads in these two necklaces designed by Elizabeth Dickinson. The single washer necklace (above) has a mother-of-pearl disc in the center. Top and center on the washer is a dash of glitter from one crystal and two silver beads. The designer used wire to wrap around the washer resulting in both a decorative and functional element. The triple-washer necklace (left) also incorporates wire as a connecting device and embellishment. More sparkle is added from sparkly varnish covering the washers as well as metallic blue seed beads. The strap is a piece of leather connected to the top, largest washer using a mounting knot.

Sea Shine Pendant
by Stephanie Lee

The coral junk, found along the beach by artist
Stephanie Lee, was the inspiration for this unusual
metal and natural-object pendant. Rather than drill
holes and possibly damage the coral, Stephanie
attached it to another found object, a piece of metal
scrap. The patina on the metal is natural, but to add
a little color to the piece, she painted the inside with
some blue acrylic paint. This gives a nice background
to the natural-colored coral piece. There were already
holes in the metal piece, so this allowed her to use
wire to strap in the coral and also attach a metal
wrapped loop at the top as the bale. For a final
touch, she added wire and bead dangles with
stamped metal tags on each end.

Fern
by Phaedra A. Torres

The "fern" in this jewelry piece is the metal leaf pin that is now a pendant in this necklace created by Phaedra A. Torres. Once a pin that might be worn by your grandmother, it is now part of a found-object necklace that also includes black-stone, gray pearls, jet Czech crystals, buttons, and suede. The whole piece is strung on beading wire and finished off with crimp beads and a sterling toggle clasp. For the buttons, Phaedra tied them on using a simple square knot technique, and arranged them randomly around the necklace strand. For the center pin, she used black suede to tie the pin and added another button to the center of the necklace.

Serpentine
by Phaedra A. Torres

Serpentine refers to the ornately carved serpentine pendant on this necklace designed and constructed by Phaedra A. Torres. Often mistaken for jade, serpentine has a similar milky-green coloring and has many of the same mystical powers attributed to it, such as protection and healing. Lucky vintage Mexican and Japanese coins are also included in this necklace, one glued to the center and the other attached to the top, along with a recycled glass bead and a polymer clay leopard-print bead. Matching green suede is attached and finished off with an overhand knot as are the bead dangles on natural-colored suede scraps.

Tibet

by Phaedra A. Torres

The dramatic silver honey jade cabochon Tibetan pendant in the center of this necklace cannot be missed. Along the sides of the pendant are also small cabochons of turquoise, jade, and coral. Designer Phaedra A. Torres incorporated similar elements in the matching necklace strand. The basic technique is stringing, using beading wire, and finishing with crimp beads and a toggle clasp. Then she tied on loads of beaded dangles with pieces of suede up and down the strand to give this a wild, bohemian look. You could imagine an ancient woman warrior wearing this as a talisman that documents her adventures. Included in the mix are serpentine, honey jade, clay beads, bone, horn, shell, copper bells, and resin pieces.

Schwinn
by Phaedra A. Torres

Aptly titled *Schwinn* for this once bicycle plate, now pendant, this unique necklace came from the imagination of mixed-media artist and jewelry maker Phaedra A. Torres. The whimsy doesn't stop with the pendant. She also added all kinds of other found objects such as buttons, a metal toy soldier, a pet tag, a key, a pop top, a coin wrapped in copper wire, and metal charms. To attach all these odds and ends, she tied on scraps of black suede lace in various places up and down the beaded necklace strand. The chunky beads include serpentine, jasper, and black-stone and are strung on beading wire and finished off with crimp beads and a sterling toggle clasp.

Layered Shrink-Plastic Art Necklace

by Lori Larson

Shrink plastic is often associated with children's crafts, but designer Lori Larson takes it to a new level in this layered art piece. Lori cut and prepared the shrink plastic using manufacturer's instructions. Then to get a distressed background, she purposefully scratched it up and rubbed it with brown chalk. To adhere the images to the plastic, she used brown ink and collaged stamp images onto the different pieces of plastic. She shrunk all the plastic pieces and then layered and glued them together. Then she covered the entire piece with resin, and added beaded dangles of metal, stone, and crystal beads. To finish off, she attached a leather strap to the holes she punched prior to shrinking.

Heritage Pillow Pin

by Julia Andrus

Julia Andrus used a photograph of her great aunt to photocopy and transfer onto fabric for this sweet pillow-style pin. The photo transferring process creates an aged look on canvas or vintage fabrics, so it automatically looks like a piece of artwork from the past. After transferring the photograph, Julia used Color Wash to give the netting an antique look, and glued on some beaded trim, which includes crystal and glass beads. Finally, she stitched the netting to the back, glued both pieces of fabric together, stuffed them with batting, and attached a pin back to complete the pin. The result is a piece of heritage she can wear with pride while she remembers her aunt.

Paper Bangle Bracelet
by Julia Andrus

Obviously, you wouldn't want to go swimming with this bracelet on after you made it. While it looks like metal and even some of the techniques used are similar to those used in metal fabrication, this bracelet designed by Julia Andrus is actually made of paper. She layered and glued strips of card stock and then pounded them with the end of a paintbrush for a hammered effect. While the glue was still drying, she formed it into a cuff and sanded the edges. It looks like metal because it is covered in copper paint. The "art" tag in the middle of the bracelet is pewter and attached using small copper rivets.

3-D Recycled Plastic Flower Earrings
by D. Lynn Reed

Silversmith and jewelry artist D. Lynn Reed combines the traditional with the unusual in these 3-D earrings. Using traditional jewelry-making materials, such as sterling silver wire and silver sheet, she fabricated the wire earring finding and the metal flower component. The unusual comes into play with her use of jelly-style plastic place mats, which she cut up and used in the center of the flower, adding both texture and color. Finally, tradition returns with the use of an 8 mm black onyx bead in the center. The bead is attached with wire, and then a wire wrap secures it to the plastic and metal flower sections.

Decorative Collage Earrings

by D. Lynn Reed

D. Lynn Reed chose the phrase "born to shop" for these colorful collage earrings. She used sterling wire and the wrapped loop technique to attach the collage element, beads, and recycled plastic together. The end of the wire continues and forms an ear hook. For the collage dangle, she used a wooden piece that she cut, drilled a hole through, and covered with gold foil, text, paint, and glitter. Finally, she covered the entire collage piece with a sealer. On the wire, she added sterling round and Bali-style spacer beads. For added color and texture, she used "jelly" place mats and cut out circular shapes, cut holes in the center, and added to the ear hooks as well.

Dictaphone Pin: 2 Asian Girls

by Jodi Bloom

Using methods of construction, then deconstruction then back to construction, designer Jodi Bloom takes pin making to a new level in this Dictaphone design. First, she makes a recording on the Dictaphone tape. Next, Jodi splatters paint on it and yanks out the tape so it falls out in streams. Finally, she adds a pin back and loads of dangle elements—vintage chain, charms, beads, and bobbles—to the once Dictaphone tape, now jewelry pin. What a great way to combine recycling and memories into a piece of jewelry!

Marry Me Earrings
by Jodi Bloom

Literally designed for a bride-to-be,
this pair of earrings created by Jodi
Bloom was the prototype for an entire
collection of jewelry designs. They combine
a luscious array of vintage and contemporary beads
dangling off multiple chains. The beads include an
assortment of materials such as crystals, glass, and
gemstones, as well as bead shapes, such as hearts
and flowers. Even the chain sections are more mix
than match. To attach the beads to the chain or to
each other, Jodi used head pins and wire, connecting
each with unwrapped loops.

Add a Horse Necklace
by Jennifer Perkins

Silver horse-head charms dangle with the aid of jump rings from the center of numerous bouquets of vintage flower pieces that artist Jennifer Perkins has gathered and assembled using head pins. The "eye" part of each pin is a perfect place to connect the jump rings and charms. The other beads are also vintage, including faceted dyed quartz bead stations in the center of the necklace. Jennifer has been collecting costume jewelry since childhood and is constantly on the lookout for unique pieces to use in her revamped vintage jewelry. Thrift stores, flea markets, and online auctions are some of her favorite hunting grounds.

Monkey Rattler
by Jennifer Perkins

Once a baby's toy, the vintage monkey rattle is now a pendant in this necklace by Jennifer Perkins. The necklace is also made up of different-size vintage polka-dot beads. Finally, she added a vintage fruit button to dangle from the center of the rattle. To help her connect items that weren't originally made for jewelry, Jennifer often must drill holes in pieces. For this, she uses a number of handheld drills, three in fact: one cordless drill, one small pen-sized drill, and one regular drill.

Quirky Bangle Bracelet
by Jennifer Perkins

Artist Jennifer Perkins mixes the old with the new in this bangle bracelet, complete with quirky flowers and dangling horse-shoe charms. She purchased the bangle and drilled holes between the polka-dot decorations. Then she layered vintage flower components together and connected them with eye pins, which she then used to dangle the charms from. While Jennifer doesn't believe there is one right or wrong way to approach found-object jewelry making, she likes to experiment with unlikely combinations. Rather than matching everything precisely, her look appears to be more random, and thus unexpected and fun.

Tiger Lou-ou Earrings
by Jennifer Perkins

Ceramic tiger beads rest on top of vintage plastic orange teardrop-shaped pendants in these earrings created by Jennifer Perkins. To help connect the tiger and teardrops, she used nested vintage flower beads connected via head pins. Jump rings at the top of each earring are used to attach the ear hooks. Jennifer looks for holes or sometimes drills her own to help connect different components together for many of her jewelry designs. Head pins, eye pins, wire, and jump rings are also useful jewelry findings for connecting all her unusual jewelry pieces together. However, she will sometimes use glue, or for items such as bracelets and rings that get a lot more wear and tear, she will use two-part epoxy.

CONTRIBUTORS

Julia Andrus (pages 41, 44, 66, 68, 71, 113, and 114) is a professional craft designer and artist who has helped develop a number of successful craft product lines, which bear her name. She has been a television moderator, author, and presenter for the arts and craft industry, and is devoted to sharing the creative spirit. Her passion is developing new products and innovative craft techniques and mingling with other artists and crafters.

julia@jadekraft.com
www.jadekraft.com

Jodi Bloom (pages 117 and 118) designs and creates all of the jewelry for So Charmed in her converted garage studio in Takoma Park, Maryland. With influences as diverse as Japanese street fashion, rock music, and popular culture, her unique work has found favor around the globe with fashionable girls of all ages. Jodi's signature beaded charm bracelets ("stories for the wrist") and other pieces are often one-of-a-kind and feature vintage materials from her vast collection.

jodi@so-charmed.com
www.so-charmed.com

Maya Brenner (page 100) designs all the jewelry for her company, Maya Brenner Designs. She is also the head designer for Luxe Jewels. Her jewelry has been featured on numerous television shows, and she has a long list of celebrity clientele, such as Debra Messing, Demi Moore, and Reese Witherspoon.

www.luxejewels.com and www.mayabrenner.com

Victoria Button (pages 28 and 60) is a Los Angeles–based designer. She uses vintage items, old pictures, found objects, and foreign treasures to create unique jewelry. Her globe-trotting history—born in Africa, raised in Australia, lived in Asia, moved to the United States—lends an international flavor to her work.

vbutton@originaljewels.com
www.originaljewels.com

Elizabeth Dickinson (pages 104 and 106) is a mixed-media artist from the United Kingdom who enjoys working with a variety of jewelry techniques and mixed-media materials. Some of her favorites include wire, shell, buttons, stone, photographs, and recycled objects.

anuraholistics@ntlworld.com

Sherri Forrester (page 97) is a self-taught jewelry designer. She has been making and selling beaded jewelry for the past seven years, is also a painter, and loves trying out new ideas.

mybloomnart@yahoo.com
www.mybloomnart.com

Elizabeth Glass Geltman and **Rachel Geltman** (page 31) are mother-and-daughter jewelry artists located in Washington, D.C. Elizabeth studied at the Art League of the Torpedo Factory, the Maryland Institute College of Art, and the Corcoran College of Art + Design. Her work is published regularly in the *Bead Bugle*, *Jewelry Arts*, and *Lapidary Journal*. She teaches a variety of courses on jewelry, including glass fusing, metal clay, wire work, and basic metalsmithing.

egeltman@starpower.net
www.geltdesigns.com

Jaimee Jo Hatt (page 99) is a designer, photographer, and entrepreneur from the San Francisco Bay area. She enjoys incorporating contrasting elements in her creations in order to manifest the potential for beautiful, peaceful coexistence among opposing polarities—the raw and refined, the playful and sophisticated, the artistic edge and simplicity.

jjo@jjodesigns.com
www.jjodesigns.com

Shannon Jefferson (page 78) is a self-taught jewelry maker from Peoria, Illinois, who loves to recycle. Her jewelry and other recycled artwork can be found in boutiques, galleries, museum shops, art fairs, and online.

project.grab.bag@insightbb.com
www.projectgrabbag.etsy.com

Carol A. Kemp (pages 101 and 103) is a mixed-media artist using paper (books), canvas, and jewelry as her substrate. She earned a bachelor's degree in theatrical design from the University of California–Santa Barbara, but it is her lifelong love and study of mythology and symbolism that have been the main source of inspiration for her work, as well as her deep inner spiritual search for truth. She teaches art and jewelry making to children and adults, and lives with her family in the central coast of California.

lifsart@verizon.net
www.lifsart.com

Lisa Lampe (pages 74 and 77) has enjoyed an array of studies in art and design. For the past six years, she has been applying her love of color and design to the sculpture of jewelry. Lisa lives in Lake Jackson, Texas, with her husband, three children, and two cats.

mail@lisalampe.com
www.lisalampe.com

Lori Larson (pages 48, 63, 83, 88, 102, and 112) is a mixed-media artist specializing in art-to-wear jewelry. Her work has appeared in several magazine publications, including *Belle Armoire Jewelry* and *Somerset Studio*. She teaches workshops nationwide.

lorilarson@gmail.com

Cyndi Lavin (page 52) is a mixed-media artist who lives and plays in central Massachusetts. Her jewelry pieces are designed for outstanding women who don't mind standing out! She also writes about jewelry making and is a frequent contibutor to *Jewelry Crafts* magazine.

cyndi@mazeltovjewelry.com
www.mazeltovjewelry.com

Stephanie Lee (pages 93 and 107) is a mixed-media artist who enjoys teaching at a growing number of national art retreats and workshops. Passionate about repurposing everyday objects, she is committed to reinventing what is common into something eclectic, expressive, and spiritually transformational.

stephanielee@uci.net
www.stephanieleestudios.bigstep.com

Theresa Mink (pages 57, 95, and 96) graduated from Houston Baptist University with degrees in art and psychology in 1983 and taught art for three years. After moving to Austin, Texas, she owned and operated a full-line home furnishing store from 1986 to 2004. Since retiring, she now concentrates on her three passions: investment management, jewelry design, and travel.

theresamink@sbcglobal.net
www.theresaminkdesigns.com

Opie and **Linda O'Brien** (pages 38 and 101) are mixed-media artists, authors, and teachers, who enjoy pushing the envelope in myriad ways, using organic, recycled, and found materials because they seem to have a voice that must be heard, a story that must be told, and a life that would otherwise be too soon forgotten. They consider themselves "caretakers of the mundane and the ordinary," and their unique offerings include books, jewelry, dolls, assemblage, and more.

gourdart@burntofferings.com
www.burntofferings.com

Yolanda Odom (page 90) is a mixed-media artist working primarily in fabric, paper, paint, beads, feathers, wood, polymer, and any other object, created or found, that catches her eye. She finds herself compelled to make and alter things, and discovers inspiration everywhere. She lives and works on the central coast of California.

syodom@yahoo.com
www.thehandandspiritstudio.com

Jennifer Perkins (pages 119, 120, and 121) is the woman behind the kitschy and irreverent jewelry website Naughty Secretary Club. She is also a founding member of the Austin Craft Mafia and a co-producer of the Stitch fashion show in Austin, Texas. Jennifer is also a co-host of *Stylelicious* and the host of *Craft Lab*, both on the DIY Network.

info@naughtysecretaryclub.com
www.naughtysecretaryclub.com

D. Lynn Reed (pages 86, 115, and 116) is a self-taught artist who enjoys exploring and experimenting with recycled materials and found objects. Through her work, she tries to encourage thought about social issues or humor and believes that adornment is a way of communicating with the world.

dlr_jewelryart@msn.com
www.modernjewelryart.com

Pam Sanders (page 34) enjoys making jewelry that has a very eclectic and ethnic flavor. She uses recycled paper, polymer clay, beads, wire, and computer images in her work.

paperpam@msn.com
www.pamsandersart.com

Gretchen S. Sarrazolla (page 98) is a happily married, proud mother of two and lives in Southern California. When she isn't in her studio working on her latest creation, Gretchen can be found singing and playing her bass guitar.

gsarrazo@sbcglobal.net
www.tiveradesigns.com

Phaedra A. Torres (pages 80, 108, 109, 110, and 111) began making jewelry as a teenager after buying a pair of earrings at a craft fair. Since then, she has been inspired by nature and other people's junk for more than fifteen years.

lluviadesigns@yahoo.com
www.lluviadesigns.com

Michela Verani (page 104) is an award-winning beading designer with innovative designs in bead stringing, Art Clay silver, glass fusing, enameling, and silver-smithing. Certified in Art Clay, Michela is an instructor as well as an Art Clay apprentice. Her work is available online as well as in various galleries.

mikki@everlastingtreasures.org
www.everlastingtreasures.org

Denise Witmer (page 105) is a professional writer and craft-o-holic. Primarily, she writes about parenting and runs the About.com Parenting Teens site. She also finds time to create and write about jewelry and scrapbooks.

dwitmer@wittyliving.com
www.wittyliving.com
parentingteens.about.com

Vickie Zumpf (page 97) lives in Montana with her husband, three children, and three grandchildren. She started making jewelry two years ago after doing photography for five years. Vickie has always enjoyed designing and creating things that make people smile.

vickiezdesigns@yahoo.com
www.vickiezdesigns.com

RESOURCES

UNITED STATES

Addicted to Rubber Stamps
800.913.2877
www.addictedtorubberstamps.com
Rubberstamping supplies

Artgems, Inc.
480.545.6009
www.artgemsinc.com
Beads, findings, and related jewelry supplies

Auntie's Beads
866.262.3237
www.auntiesbeads.com
Beads and general jewelry-making supplies

Beadalon
866.423.2325
www.beadalon.com
Beading wire, memory wire, and general jewelry supplies

The Bead Shop
650.383.3434
www.beadshop.com
Beads, jewelry-making supplies, kits, DVDs, and CDs

The Bead Warehouse
301.565.0487
www.thebeadwarehouse.com
Stone beads and general jewelry-making supplies

B'Sue Boutiques
www.bsueboutiques.com
General beading supplies and metal stampings

CGM
800.426.5246
www.cgmfindings.com
Wholesale wire, metal beads, and findings

D.D. Hess
615.548.4140
www.ddhess.com
Glass tags, lampwork beads, and fused glass products

Dick Blick Art Materials
800.828.4548
www.dickblick.com
General craft supplies

Gemshow Online Jewelry Supply
877.805.7440
www.gemshow-online.com
Crystals, metal beads, and findings

Environmental Technologies Inc.
707.443.9323
www.eti-usa.com
Consumer and industrial products for resin casting, including Envirotex Lite

Fire Mountain Gems and Beads
800.423.2319
www.firemountaingems.com
General jewelry-making supplies, books, and displays

HHH Enterprises
800.777.0218
www.hhhenterprises.com
General jewelry-making supplies

Jade Kraft
801.733.4716
www.jadekraft.com
Supplies for bookmaking, scrapbooking, and mixed-media artwork

Jan's Jewels
405.840.2341
www.jansjewels.com
General jewelry-making supplies

Land of Odds
615.292.0610
www.landofodds.com
General jewelry-making supplies and seed beads

Monsterslayer
505.598.5322
www.monsterslayer.com
Metal findings, wire, and beads

Ornametea.com
919.834.6260
www.ornamentea.com
Mixed-media jewelry, fiber beads, and related supplies

Out on a Whim
800.232.3111
www.whimbeads.com
Seed beads, crystals, and findings

Rings & Things
800.366.2156
www.rings-things.com
Wholesale jewelry-making supplies

Rio Grande
800.545.6566
www.riogrande.com
Equipment, beads, metal, and other related jewelry supplies

The Scrap Bucket
972.612.7200
www.thescrapbucketonline.com
Scrapbook services and supplies

Scrapbooking Supplies R Us
800.352.1980
www.scrapbookingsuppliesrus.com
Embellishments, albums, and related scrapbooking accessories

Scrapbooking Warehouse
831.768.1810
www.scrapbooking-warehouse.com
Scrapbooking and rubberstamp products

Shipwreck Beads
360.754.2323
www.shipwreckbeads.com
General jewelry-making supplies

Soft Flex Company
866.925.3539
www.softflextm.com
Soft Flex beading wire and general jewelry-making supplies

South Pacific Wholesale Co.
800.338.2162
www.beading.com
Stone beads and general jewelry-making supplies

Stampington & Company
877.782.6737
www.stampington.com
Rubberstamp and paper-arts products

Suze Weinberg Design Studio
732.493.1390
www.schmoozewithsuze.com
Rubberstamping supplies and resources

Urban Maille Chainworks
303.838.7432
www.urbanmaille.com
Precision-cut precious-metal jump rings, kits, and tools

Wire-Sculpture.com
601.636.0600
www.wire-sculpture.com
Wire, beads, and general jewelry supplies

INTERNATIONAL

African Trade Beads
www.africantradebeads.com
*UK supplier of Czech, seed, and various
imported beads*

Aussie Scrapbooking Studio
+61.02.9873.1750
www.scrapbookingstudio.com
General scrapbooking supplies

The Bead Company of Australia
+61.02.9546.4544 ext. 25
www.beadcompany.com.au
Beads and general jewelry-making supplies

The Bead Shop
+44.0127.374.0777
www.beadsunlimited.co.uk
UK supplier of beads and related supplies

Beadfx
877.473.2323
www.beadfx.com
Canadian supplier of glass, crystal, and seed beads

Beadgems
+44.0845.123.2743
www.beadgems.com
UK supplier of beads and jewelry supplies

Beadworks
+44.0207.240.0931
www.beadshop.co.uk
UK supplier of general beading supplies

Canadian Beading Supply
800.291.6668
www.canbead.com
Wholesale and retail bead and jewelry supplier

Gem Craft
+44.0161 477 0435
www.gemcraft.co.uk
Gem and mineral supplier

Hobbycraft
Stores throughout the United Kingdom
+44.0120.259.6100
Bead shop and jewelry-making supplier

House of Orange
250.483.1468
www.houseoforange.biz
Canadian supplier of beads and related jewelry supplies

Katie's Treasures
+61.02.4956.3435
www.katiestreasures.com.au
Australian supplier of beads and related jewelry supplies

Kernowcrafts Rocks and Gems Limited
+44.0187.257.3888
www.kernowcraft.com
UK supplier of gems, crystals, and jewelry supplies

Mee Ngai Wah in Sham Shui Po
+852.8171.3226
(fax) +852.8171.3312
*Wholesale and retail jewelry supplies from Hong
Kong*

Scrapbook Super Store
+61.02.4722.2152
www.scrapbooksuperstore.com.au
General scrapbooking supplies

Spacetrader Beads
+61.03.9534.6867
www.spacetrader.com.au
Australian supplier of beads and related jewelry supplies

ABOUT THE AUTHOR

Tammy Powley is a writer and designer. She is the author of a number of jewelry books including *Making Designer Gemstone and Pearl Jewelry, Making Designer Bead and Wire Jewelry*, and *Making Designer Seed Bead, Stone, and Crystal Jewelry*, all from Quarry Books. Tammy also writes for numerous digital media, and you can find links to all of her online writings on her website, www.tammypowley.com. In addition to studying a variety of jewelry techniques, from beading to metalsmithing, she has worked extensively with fused glass, fibers, and paper art. After spending eight years on the art show circuit, she eventually turned to writing about art, though she continues to sell her work through commissions. Tammy resides in Port St. Lucie, Florida, with her husband, Michael, and a house full of dogs and cats.

ACKNOWLEDGMENTS

The mixed-media jewelry artists who contributed their time and talents to this book are an unbelievably generous and professional group of people. They answered my zillion and one questions, and put up with my "need it ASAP" demands. Because of their imaginative approach to jewelry making, they helped make this book a reality.

To the Quarry crew—Mary Ann Hall and Rochelle Bourgault—thank you for your guidance, hard work, and expertise. To the other members of Quarry Books who work behind the scenes—those talented folks in photography, design, and illustration—I know I can always count on all of you to produce a quality product that is as much a piece of art as the jewelry pictured within.

Finally, I thank my family, including my husband, Michael, and our furry menagerie. You always help me de-stress during deadline time and understand when I disappear into my office for days at a time.